Praise for *My Wild and Sleepless Nights*

reality of motherhood, this ...
Emma Beddie...

'What does being a mother really feel like? Clover Stroud's powerhouse of a memoir gets closer than anything else I have read to answering that question . . . Buy it, read it, and enjoy it for the wild ride it is.' Alice O'Keeffe, *Guardian*

'Clover Stroud's brilliantly unvarnished memoir finds the heroism and poetry in having kids . . . Much of this book reads like a nature memoir, full of landscape both external and internal . . . How brilliant for someone to write about the blankness as well as the beauty.' Nell Frizzell, *Telegraph*

'Clover Stroud charts the highs and lows of motherhood in all their deep, dark glory.' Sarra Manning, *RED* Magazine

'Rare are the books about motherhood, rarer still; the true, the generous, tender, resonant ones. This is that book. I loved it and I love Clover's voice.' Sophie Dahl

'Clover Stroud writes with precise intimacy and fearless honesty. She has somehow found a wholly original way to describe motherhood and, in doing so, truly conveys what it's like, in all its messy, sexy glory.' Hadley Freeman

'This is quite simply the best book about motherhood I have ever read: touching, tender, honest and true . . . Bliss and boredom coexist side by side – and the contradictions are at the core of it all. Stroud's book will give anyone heading out on this fearsome journey a lantern to guide the way.' Eleanor Mills, *Sunday Times*

'I have been waiting for a book like this for a long time. Stroud captures the very essence of motherhood in all its contradictions . . . There are few other books about motherhood as brave, honest and beautifully written as this one.' Sarah Langford, author of *In Your Defence*

Clover Stroud is a writer and journalist writing for the *Daily Mail*, *Sunday Times*, *Daily Telegraph* and *Condé Nast Traveler* among others. She lives in Oxfordshire with her husband and five children. Her first book, *The Wild Other*, was shortlisted for the Wainwright Prize.

My Wild and Sleepless Nights

A Mother's Story

CLOVER STROUD

doubleday

TRANSWORLD PUBLISHERS
Penguin Random House, One Embassy Gardens,
8 Viaduct Gardens, London SW11 7BW
www.penguin.co.uk

Transworld is part of the Penguin Random House group of companies
whose addresses can be found at global.penguinrandomhouse.com

Penguin
Random House
UK

First published in Great Britain in 2020 by Doubleday
an imprint of Transworld Publishers
Paperback edition published 2021

A CIP catalogue record for this book
is available from the British Library.

ISBN
9781784164119

Typeset in Bembo Std by Integra Software Services Pvt. Ltd, Pondicherry.
Printed and bound in Great Britain by Clays Ltd, Elcograf S.p.A.

The authorized representative in the EEA is Penguin Random House Ireland,
Morrison Chambers, 32 Nassau Street, Dublin D02 YH68.

Penguin Random House is committed to a sustainable
future for our business, our readers and our planet. This book
is made from Forest Stewardship Council® certified paper.

For Jimmy, Dolly, Evangeline, Dash, Lester.
Here's looking at you, kids.

Prologue

With the monitor hooked around my belly like a seat belt, I can hear the heartbeat of my unborn baby galloping along inside me like the tiny hooves of a miniature horse. It's breathing with me, the pulse so much more real than any of the watery scans I had at twelve, twenty, thirty weeks, which just looked like moving snowstorms. Those hooves of heartbeat are fast and persistent, and in between each small, perfect beat I feel my own huge, messy life realizing itself. The galloping heartbeat sounds ancient and wild, so different from the controlled, institutional medical authority surrounding me. 'NOW WASH YOUR HANDS', demands a bright yellow sign by the sink in the corner of the room, as if the sign itself were standing there, hands on hips, waiting, just as I do with my younger children when they refuse to brush their teeth.

I'm thirty-eight weeks pregnant, that moment in this forty-week marathon when pregnancy feels like a practical joke I've played on myself that's gone badly wrong. It's lost the urgency of eight, thirteen, twenty-one, thirty-two weeks, and now is an experience that's endless, holding me stiller and stiller as my belly tightens, a huge, hot, heavy presence that accompanies me everywhere and that's really not that much fun. I had been worried the baby was too still, hiccupping less, rummaging around inside me with less insistence. And this is my fifth baby, so the stakes are high. I've rolled the dice and it's fallen dazzlingly well in my favour four times over the past fifteen years: Jimmy, Dolly, Dash and Evangeline. Sometimes I think much of my life has been about seeking strong motion both to make me feel alive and distract from the pain of existence. I have found that strong motion through adrenalin and danger, or drugs, or sex, but none of those comes close to the wild feeling of emerging from the brink of labour, blood pouring from me, my body split open, holding new life in my arms.

I don't want to leave the hospital to go home to the other children or to Pete, to the demands which send me running around the house in circles, finding hundreds of shoes, poking small feet into rolled-up socks, draining soft broccoli, mopping up splashed milk, incessantly negotiating with adolescents about whose house I will drive them to and what sort of cereal I will buy later, looking at Year 7 maths homework I don't understand, chasing small, slippery, wet bodies out of the bath and into their pyjamas, then back down the stairs next morning to do it all again and again. I want to stay cocooned here, soft and quiet, imagining the baby who will soon arrive, listening to his or her heartbeat, while sleeping, resting, absolving myself from my job as a mother to my children at home, just for a few hours. When I'm ready, there will still be time to wash and fold muslin squares, and pull the zipped-up suitcase of old baby clothes out of the attic, wash the sheets of the Moses basket, press drops of lavender oil into a small knitted blanket that's somehow made its way across time from my mother's hands when I was a baby. There will be time to pack a hospital bag with disposable pants and those old-fashioned sanitary towels you can bleed and bleed into, and miniature newborn nappies so small Evangeline will use them for her toy dolls. There will be time for all these things, but now the hospital room is calm, the baby's heartbeat a hypnotic passport to sleep.

My phone rings. I slip the monitor down my bump, fishing into the bag for the phone. It's Jimmy's school. I ignore the call, but the call will not be ignored.

The woman's voice is tight with urgency, insisting I need to come into school immediately. I stare at the gel on my huge stomach, basically the only thing I can see, blocking my view of my feet, or the end of the bed, or anything beyond it. My abdomen, right now, seems to fill the entire room.

'I can't come to school immediately. I'm having a baby soon, next week maybe,' I say, even though this sounds ridiculous. 'I'm actually having a scan right now.'

I think she'll understand.

'Miss Stroud, you need to come into school now,' she repeats. I sense her frowning at me through the telephone.

'Is everything all right? Can you tell me what's going on? Is Jimmy OK?'

She tells me that Jimmy is OK. 'But due to student confidentiality I can't tell you more, except that you must come into school.'

Confusion and a little anger rise through me: there should be no student confidentiality, since this is my *child* we are talking about. For a moment a feeling of horror passes through me, the prospect that Jimmy might have done something really awful, but it doesn't seem possible, since this is Jimmy we are talking about. Jimmy, my first child, who tells me everything, who would not lie to me, who still kisses me on the lips when he leaves for school every morning, and still ends calls with 'love you, Mum'.

The baby gallops on. And suddenly I have a strong urge to throw the monitor and phone on to the ground and run barefoot out of here, away from everyone, my unborn baby and my four children and my husband. This wasn't supposed to be the emotion of today, and of these last moments of pregnancy. This was supposed to be the day I started taking it easy, giving myself space to enjoy these last days. It was supposed to be the time I started actually visualizing the baby, breathing into the end of the pregnancy to see my uterus and cervix and vulva like a flower expanding into life.

I suggest I could come in this afternoon, after the baby has been fully monitored, or tomorrow morning, inflecting my voice to make it sound helpful. She interrupts. 'It's a safeguarding issue,' she says, but something in the tone of her voice tells me it's not my son's safety she is guarding.

Less than an hour later I'm searching for a place in a crowded school car park, and signing in to school, as if visiting a prisoner. Heat seeps from my body, and because I am so hot and so huge, there's no way I look anything like efficient, or on-the-case, or even that parental, which is odd, considering I am thirty-eight weeks pregnant.

By contrast, the headmistress, waiting for me in her office, looks severe in a sharp pencil skirt and heels, her hair swept on top of her head. She also looks quite hot. No one says anything as I pull my huge belly into the room. Sitting at the table is my son. Jimmy's fifteen years are worn so heavily on him, his blond hair a fuzz across his face, his expression furious and defiant. And I have to assume that the Tupperware box in front of him which contains a handful of perfectly rolled joints must be the reason we're here.

They can't be *his* though, because Jimmy would have told me. He is my first child and we have no secrets.

In that moment the whole kaleidoscope of motherhood shifts. Have I been completely blind? Did I really not notice anything? And has Jimmy got a secret life that he has been applying all of his wit and originality to hiding from me, for weeks, months, maybe even years?

I feel a plummeting, twisted dread that those joints on the table are not just about having a quick puff behind the bike sheds, but the start of a thin-end-of-a-wedge crisis that will end up in a filthy bedsit with greying nylon curtains and a needle in the arm of a sweaty, trembling boy.

I open and close my mouth, trying to focus, like a comedy fish. Jimmy won't look at me. I try to work out how we have got here. I try not to cry.

I *do* cry, though. At this point in my pregnancy, the opening chord of a certain song on the radio will make me cry, and the sight of a fragment of a green shirt my mother dressed me in as a baby will make me cry, and even the chance to lie down in a dark room without anyone pressing small, sticky palms into my face, or asking me to find their lunch box, will make me cry. And today, the baby and its tiny precious heartbeat are forgotten as I hear the words leave the headmistress's mouth: the school has a zero-tolerance drugs policy, there will be consultations with independent educational consultants and social workers, and a managed move to a new school.

Jimmy looks down at his bitten nails, the baby kicks me below the ribs, and then all three of us are being herded out of the door into the blinking summer heat.

As we drive home, I cry again, then I shout, and my voice cracks when Jimmy shouts back, punching the dashboard and trying to get out of the car while I'm driving, and I have to grab his sweatshirt to yank him to safety. It's a fast, physical commotion, hot like petrol fumes that might ignite and blow us apart. There is so much anger and failure and it's directed right at me so that I'm spun around inside myself, disorientated about where I am as a mother.

Something unsaid is tearing us apart. Motherhood and being a son and individual responsibility and fear are suddenly all mixed up together, so that we're both blaming each other about whose fault this actually is.

Because although I'm furious and I'm hurt that this is happening, I'm not really surprised. I'm also confused and very tired, but I try to ignore these feelings, so I can instead remain focused on the challenge ahead.

This doesn't really work. I'm overwhelmed. And after that I don't know *what* to feel. I'm angriest with myself. I know exactly what it's like to want to escape into the enticing world of getting high. And I've been Jimmy's age. I always thought that when this moment arrived, I'd have seen it coming and anticipated it. I thought I'd be prepared. Cool, even. Not snotty and furious, mocked by mascara panda blotches.

When we get home, Jimmy rages out of the car as Dash and Evangeline swarm from the house towards me across the lawn, pinning themselves against me as they clamour for me to hold their faces close to mine and to listen to the all-important news of what they had for lunch and their latest scrapes and grazes. They are a swirling, spinning merry-go-round, and I try to cover the sides of their heads in kisses, to shore up against unknown future ruin, while at the same time not wanting to lose sight of Jimmy's vanishing, furious shoulders.

And I think of the way people react when they see I'm pregnant with a fifth child. Usually what they say is: 'You're brave! Are you mad?'

I wonder if they might have a point.

I go to Jimmy's room but he won't open the door.

'You're always busy. You don't – ever – listen. Ever. I wish you'd just fuck off and leave me alone anyway,' he screams through the door. 'You're always distracted by the kids. You don't even know who I am! How do you think you can look after another baby? Just GO AWAY!'

I say we need to talk but he carries on shouting. The supine days of late pregnancy that I dreamed of vanish like a mirage, evaporating in the summer heat as my brain spins like a fruit machine of exhausting, flashing emotion about what happens next. Most of all I feel stupid, as well as massive, standing outside Jimmy's room, trying to speak to him through the door and maintain any dignity or authority as a parent at all.

In the kitchen, Dolly, alert to a crisis unfolding around her older brother, is keeping order by preparing toast and cups of milk for Dash and Evangeline. She looks a little tentative, but she's smiling, long hair falling around her shoulders, gliding where the younger children dart, and somehow managing to make her blue nylon uniform look both stylish and attractive.

'Did you have a good day, Mum?' she says, sounding bright, as all the children love it when one of the others is in trouble, until I look up at her, smiling thinly, and she sees my blotched face. 'Mum, are you OK? Mum? Have you been crying? Mum?'

1

Two Blue Lines

When I first calculated that the baby would be born in the middle of July, in high summer, I saw the final days of pregnancy as a time when I could stop running. I thought about going to a store to buy some proper recliners with cushions for the garden, rather than just lying on a rug I'd ripped from the sofa. I imagined that in these last days I'd be outside with the children as they played on the lawn. The end of every pregnancy was usually such a blur of work that needed to be finished, or walls that needed to be painted, but this time I'd told myself I really would let those things go in the final days, and concentrate on the only thing that really mattered, which was the baby, the new person who would soon arrive.

And nine months earlier, when my period was late and I went to buy a pregnancy test, vaguely wondering if I'd kept Dash's buggy and whether we still had a

Moses basket, drugs and expulsion and an angry head-mistress were not on my mind.

The pregnancy is not a shock. I have wanted it, but it does not make me feel especially happy or for that matter sad. It has changed me, though. I know with a terrible sort of inevitability that I don't need to spend eleven pounds on two Clear Blue tests. I know, just from the way my breasts feel, tight and excitable when I fold my arms across my chest, that I am different, that I am now two pulses not one, doubly alive.

Pregnancy makes me aware of every moment that passes, while also heavy with a soupy apprehension about what I've just done to our lives. I have known for a week, since, standing in front of the long mirror in our room, I unhooked my bra and watched it fall to the ground in the late-night silence of our bedroom. My breasts, with a tracing of blue veins like deep-water rivers pressed against the white skin, were changed, almost as if they were breathing in a way that was separate from the rest of my body and so had taken on their own life. I squeezed my nipple until it made me gasp, a feeling that was raw and animal, like the sex, three weeks before, which had made me feel as if my entire body and being was open and consuming itself. That kind of sex was a sort of trance, a losing of myself and becoming a part of him: it was everything I wanted. And it contained a primal energy so that all the sex we'd ever had together was present in that one act. It was almost violent, although I'd felt not so much like a black widow spider, consuming my mate through sex, but more like a marsupial antechinus, fucking myself into oblivion.

'Do you mind either way?' The woman behind the till has scanned my box of Colgate and bottle of nit shampoo, but her hand pauses over the pregnancy test. My eyes flick quickly up to hers. I have four children already; asking me if I mind, as I buy a test that will seal my fate, feels way too intimate. What if I had been a different person, in different circumstances, and I'd replied: Yes, I really do, my boyfriend has said he'll leave if we have another baby. Or: Yes, I really do, I've had eight miscarriages and this is my last try; if it's negative I think I might die of sadness. Somehow the pregnancy test makes me public property. And if the stick does turn blue, complete strangers will soon want to cup their hands over my belly, touching a part of me that feels private.

'I'll be happy if it's positive,' I reply, smiling at her quickly, pretending, as I often do in motherhood, that I'm in control, when what I really want to tell her is that I'm scared, because this is life and death, isn't it? The oblong box might look innocuous, but my fate, and possibly that of another, sits inside it. And even though I have four children, I have also had three miscarriages and felt the almost biological sense of loneliness they brought with them. Should I say to this lady behind the till: Can you tell me, is this a risk I should be taking?

Instead I stuff the pregnancy test into the bottom of my bag, wrapped up in its white and blue bag, and smile at her quickly before leaving. Later that evening, across the sea of coloured plastic Lego and plates of sugary carbohydrate that Evangeline and Dash blanket the kitchen in, I ask Jimmy to reach for my phone charger in my bag, forgetting the pregnancy arsenal in there too.

'Really, Mum?' he says, holding up the test, shielded within my bag, as if it's something illicit or shocking he must hide from Dolly and his younger siblings. 'Really?' He gives me a look of weary disapproval, as though he is the tired parent, chastising, chivvying, shocked.

'Why on earth would you do that to yourself?' a woman at a party asks me, a week later, when I tell her how many children I have. I don't even say I'm pregnant. It's a work event in London, with waiters bearing lonely canapés through the carpeted bowels of a central-London hotel. The woman has a faint American accent, close-cut brown hair and tortoiseshell glasses matching her shiny brogues. I have rushed to get here, peeling the children from me and flinging Dash into Pete's arms, so that I arrive sweaty and frizzy and feeling flayed. Maybe she's sensing some defensiveness about my reproductive choices. She smiles, putting her hand over the rim of her wine glass to stop the waiter hovering there, and tips her head to one side, politely, for my answer.

How do you explain why you have four or even five children to someone for whom the idea of anything more than one, two maximum, is absolutely mystifying? We have two boys and two girls – so neat, people say, that symmetry. There's no reason to have another baby, apart from a ravenous kind of hunger that's like joy and melancholy and nostalgia and daring all mixed together.

What I want to say is this: The reason I'd do this to myself is because I want messy. And I'm greedy. And I want another one because four makes me feel neat. Neat is so unfamiliar it makes me feel homesick, but creating messiness is like making it right. Because even though there will be less of the good things, like sleep, time, sex and money, there'll also be more pure love and I want to wrap that around me every day I can while I'm alive on this earth. Because being pregnant makes me feel sexual and engaged in a way that often I don't. Because I can. Because I want to test my body with the biggest physical challenge I know how to wilfully bring upon it, and because I want to touch the actual brink of death as I know I will do in childbirth. Because I don't want my life to be easy – I don't want a quiet life. Because my eldest child is a teenager and that's made me see how terrified I really am of this thing called motherhood ending. And also because motherhood hurts, and I like being hurt. Sometimes, when I'm having sex, I like to be hit.

But I don't say any of that because a mother can't say these things.

So instead I say: 'Well, I'm one of five, so I think there's something in me that's always wanted that sense of big, colourful chaos, with lots of siblings.' Then I pause, trying to make a little joke. 'I like the thought of mess.'

For quite a lot of my late-adolescent and early-adult life, I'd attempt to imagine what it would be like to do a pregnancy test when you really wanted it to be positive, rather than willing with every atom of your being that one line would appear in the little window, and not two. I thought it would feel like the moment I stopped anticipating life and actually started inhabiting it or even enjoying it. I also thought that doing a positive pregnancy test when you want a baby might be tender and even romantic.

'You've got to be kidding, Clover.' Pete's face slides downwards when I stand in front of him in our room, holding out the pregnancy-test box.

A rare moment: the house is still and silent and we're alone. I am as apprehensive as he is. Having another baby will be like letting a wild animal into our life. Because although I want the mess, the reality is also terrifying and disorientating. I really, really want this baby. I must have it. But it will also take up so much of my brain, my life and my time, that however much I want it, I know that another child will stop me having the thoughts I want to have, and, to a great extent, living the life that I want to lead. I know, too, that motherhood can bring a sort of violent, overwhelming love that feels like being encased in metal and dropped into a deep silent sea. This mother love can feel as raw and rare as cutting through the soft dark crimson of uncooked liver, and as unsettling as that, too. These are the reasons why another pregnancy isn't pure joy.

'Oh God, oh God, oh my God!' Pete says when I show him the two lines. 'I mean, it's amazing, incredible.' He buries his head in his hands; then he laughs. 'What a nightmare! An amazing nightmare!' Then he reaches out to me, enclosing me in his arms, the safest place in the world I know – the best place, too, because he's so up for life, he's never scared. 'Five! Five children! What the fuck is that going to be like?'

*

The feeling of sickness that slides over me in the early afternoon, every day, is as claustrophobic as putting my head in a plastic bag. I leave my desk and crawl on to the sofa, face down in a cushion, until it's passed. I cannot even look out of the window: white clouds scudding across the sky remind me of being in the back of a car as a child, of motion sickness. I'm tired, too, a soupy blanket of exhaustion so intense it's as if I have swallowed a pill and the drug has seeped into every part of my body, even my fingertips and strands of hair.

The midwife says I should include a lot of whole grains and oily fish in my diet. I nod a silent lie to her over my blue notes, because I know these things will make me want to throw up from a very dark and deep place inside me. At the supermarket, bags of watercress and spinach salad look toxic. A salad I've carefully prepared ends face down in the bin.

What I crave instead is the fast oblivion of processed white food: toast and butter made from the cheapest sliced bread, pints of full-fat milk, Rich Tea biscuits and bowls of Weetabix crusted with white sugar. I'm ashamed of what I eat in front of anyone but Dash, my wide-eyed toddler and partner in crime. I drop Evangeline for four half-days a week at pre-school, and then I take Dash, clutching a handful of coloured trains, to the Co-op, where we sit with our shopping in the car outside, eating cheap sausage rolls. At supper when Dash starts screaming because there's broccoli on his plate beside the chicken, I find myself much more for-giving than I would have been a few weeks before, more patient as I start a new plate for him, since if spinach touched my plate I might start screaming in the same way, too.

Early evening and I am lying pinned on the bed by the exhaustion of early pregnancy, with Dash and Evangeline, exhausted from childhood, on either side. In the next room, I can hear Dolly watching music videos on YouTube, and further down the corridor, Jimmy is having a conversation while gaming with someone on the other side of the world, breaking into different accents and then cracking into raucous laughter. Without even going into his bedroom, I know he'll be leaning back, precariously balanced on one of the green-painted wooden kitchen chairs, which will soon break.

Evangeline demands that I read her a story about a hamster living on a barge, while Dash shrieks about wanting a Jesus story. Willing to do anything to stop the screaming, I agree to both, although it will postpone sleep yet further. I am so tired, the words on the page fall over one another into a single sentence. I try skipping the adjectives, then potentially important sentences, and finally entire paragraphs, without the children noticing, desperate for the day to finish so that I can close my throbbing eyes.

Evangeline jolts me as I fall asleep. Dash has not noticed; he's making train tracks in his duvet. 'I don't want you to read the words anyway,' she says, her breath warm, smelling of Digestive biscuits. 'I just want you to look at my face.' She stops and a quiet smile traces over her features. 'And I was thinking I might be old enough for a pet of my own. A hamster or a rabbit of my very own.' She pauses, trying to register anything on my face, brightening when she meets no resistance. 'Yes, I think you might,' I mumble, closing my eyes again. 'Let's talk about it tomorrow.' By 7.56 p.m. I'm asleep on the single bed in the room she shares with Dash.

Dolly's face crumples, her eyes glistening, when we tell her and Jimmy about the baby. Dolly's emotions are always on the surface, always present. Everything about her is pure heart. 'Oh, Mum, that's so amazing,' she cries, pressing her face into my shoulder. I think she really means it. She was just a little girl when Evangeline was born but mothering is something she does intuitively, generously, with her younger siblings. 'It's so funny. I never thought I'd have so many brothers and sisters.'

We haven't told anyone about the pregnancy for weeks: partly because our family is such a palpable chaos that having a conversation alone is very rarely possible, but also because having a secret Pete and I alone share is valuable. And I'm superstitious, and not talking about the pregnancy makes those early, tentative weeks pass faster.

Jimmy merely raises his eyebrows. He knew, of course he knew, as soon as he saw the pregnancy test in my bag. But he hugs me, telling me it will be great, and really sweet to have another baby in the family. But it's difficult, too, as they both know that a new baby doesn't spell straightforward pleasure and happiness. More babies are a joy, a sweet, jolly, milky blessing, everything like that, but they will separate Pete and me from Jimmy and Dolly once again, slicing up the moments of time we have to give to one another, the energy and attention we have to devote to one another. New babies create new chaos; all of us know that well.

I was thirty-four, living in Oxford, when I met Pete. Jimmy and Dolly were nine and six and we were close in a special way; I'd split up with their father after Dolly was born and while Jimmy was still almost a toddler. Most nights, the three of us tangled together to sleep; absolute single motherhood was financially terrifying but filled my heart and my head with complete love. We were as close as it's possible to be, a band of three, since their father was luminously important in their lives but mostly absent. He'd take them to stay with his parents for some weekends and part of the holidays, but the work and the fun of bringing them up fell almost entirely to me.

When Pete and I fell in love, my family shifted, and then resettled. Pete's heart is huge, his love is absolute, and he wrapped it around the children as much as me. I'd never wanted that from anyone since I'd split from their father, but with Pete I saw a way of doing family as a brand-new band of four that was both cosy and exciting. There was a relief, and novelty, too, in sharing the parenting.

Pete could carry both children in his arms at the same time to lift them out of a swimming pool, and I no longer had to lie about the children's ages when I took them to the zoo, pretending they were younger than they were to get them in free. Buying a family ticket was a sweet new experience. He took an interest in the team sports I ignored, ferrying Jimmy to

cricket club on the other side of town and playing
football with him in the park when the nights got
longer. He'd turn maths homework into a game for
Dolly, and read aloud to her after school when she was
diagnosed with acute dyslexia. Holidays together were
a new joy; we bought a dilapidated convertible for
eight hundred pounds from a neighbour and drove
through France with the roof down while the children shivered and shrieked with excitement in the
back. Pete cared, a great deal. He didn't want to replace
their father, but was always generous about the time
he gave them both. It was a new delight to meet a
man who was not scared by my family life. My children, my baggage, were an important part of the thing
he loved about me.

I felt as close to my two children and Pete as it's possible to be.

As our family grew, Pete's commitment to Jimmy
and Dolly did not diminish. He brought Jimmy and
Dolly to hospital to meet the newborn Evangeline,
holding Dolly's hand close as she peered around the
ward curtains to meet her new sister for the first time,
her face flushed with emotion. He laughed and did not
chastise when Jimmy swung, precariously, on the end
of the hospital bed. Closeness is what Pete has always
wanted, for our family and our shared children to really
care for each other.

Of course, there were parts of parenting Dolly and
Jimmy that always fell to me: discipline and parents'
evening were my responsibility, but if he did feel a
different kind of love for Evangeline than for them, he
has never shown it. I watched, alert, but he portioned

out his love as equally as it's possible to do when toddlers battled for attention, bombing us like screeching
seagulls, while Jimmy and Dolly swooped ahead. My
band of three became our band of four and then five,
and, soon after, six, when Dash was born. Life got
messier, noisier, funnier. But the new, big family also
brought newer, bigger responsibilities. We spilled out
of the house Jimmy, Dolly and I had been living in
when I met Pete, into the countryside, to a house
with a garden and fields all around it, where there was
space for us all. We had our own bedrooms and two
bathrooms, but the move from Oxford also made life
more complicated, too. Pete spent more time away,
working to support these children he adored. We'd
had children to manifest the love that we felt for each
other, but now the responsibility of that meant, at
least for most of the week, we were often living apart,
while he was in London, or abroad on business. And I
was the parent the children turned to for help, since I
was always there.

Fitting my work around the scramble of family life
occupies me a lot of the time. I was a single mother to
Dolly and Jimmy until they were seven and ten, and
my income supported us alone. I said yes to every single piece of work I was offered and I made mothering
and working fit together; the only way I could make
that work was by employing au pairs. I was self-
employed, and when I was on my own with just Jimmy
and Dolly, I'd struggled to afford nursery. Instead, my
children slept in bed with me and a series of au pairs
used the spare room in our tiny, two-bedroom house.
The juggle of working and caring for children is

difficult for all mothers. I think juggling is the wrong word, too, since it makes the intensely fraught puzzle of having a working life and being present as a mother sound playful, even fun, when it's neither of these things. The plates fall and smash all the time. I'm constantly on the run, grabbing moments to work which I feel I've stolen from my children. The school assemblies I missed, the concerts I was late to, the parents' evenings I had to reorganize are the guilty price I pay: and make no mistake, it's a price.

Over the years, au pairs have come in and out of our life; when it works it's a mutually supportive relationship which can become a friendship. They get out of it a home and bed and the chance to learn English while being paid, and I get an extra pair of hands to help poke little limbs into pyjama tops, throw toast on to plates in the chaos of the morning, read to one child while I'm bathing another, ferry them to baby groups or push the back of a swing while I'm on a deadline. Sometimes the au pairs have stayed with my family as long as a year; sometimes they walk into the kitchen, blink at the glare of noise and motion, then leave hours later. It takes a certain kind of person to enjoy the colour and mess of a big family in the middle of the countryside. Most au pairs would prefer a family with two children at school and a Tube stop close to the Central line. The help we have is a rough jigsaw which sometimes all slots neatly into place, but often simply falls apart. It's a scramble, all the time.

And this is why the news of another baby is not a straightforward joy. It will bring deep love with it, and also more bills to pay, more separation, and certainly more sleepless nights.

'It's always the same, even though I know another baby would be completely impractical,' my friend Kathryn tells me as a tightness settles into her usually animated features. 'It's this sense I have that something important is over for me. It's not just that I'll never hold another baby who's actually mine, who I carried and gave birth to, but a feeling that something inside me is unfinished, like a song I can't sing any more.' We'd been trying to meet for a coffee or a walk for eight months, something so simple which had eluded us because of work that needed attention, or children suddenly sick off school. She pushes her plate away and rakes her fingers through the brown hair that's falling across her face, pulling the curls back, controlling them determinedly in a grip. 'I'll never be a mother like that, to a newborn, to a baby, again.'

For a second I see her in a flash of memory as I first did, in a breastfeeding clinic in Oxford, when Evangeline was a baby, our daughters born within two weeks of one another. She was luminous with a bliss that wiped out the exhaustion and physical demands of a difficult birth and a baby who struggled to feed. Since then, we've spent afternoons together, our toddlers a blur at our feet as we dissected the feelings of new motherhood and the lives we had before, which seemed to have gone. When I was pregnant with Dash, I felt something new, a tension that had never been there before arising between us, because Kathryn wanted another child, but her boyfriend didn't. He already has a daughter from a previous relationship who lives with him and Kathryn, and feels complete.

'I know that another baby would be totally impractical,' she repeats, leaning back in her chair. 'But this strange ache has never stopped, not once, for the past few years. He says the end of parenting is in sight, like it's this awful thing that we both want to end. I get that. Parenting is hard; it's relentless. It doesn't give you any space. And I know that he has a point. We can't fit into our house as it is. We can't afford it. He's right. But none of those arguments take away these feelings that I need to mother a baby again.'

I shift in my chair, pulling my shirt from my front, leaning forward into the table and offering consoling words about the joy she must be getting from her daughter, and the time and attention she can lavish on her, and how these things are so evident in the bright, happy little girl she is bringing up. I do not say anything to her about my pregnancy. Not now. At this moment, there are things that cannot be said. I am separated from another woman, my friend, because I cannot talk about this part of motherhood: the wanting and then the getting and the resenting and the missing, the longing. Motherhood has put us at odds with one another.

Almost like clockwork, as my second trimester arrives at thirteen weeks, the cloak of tiredness and nausea is shrugged off and replaced by a power pack I slip on every morning after an unusually deep sleep, which gives me the sense I am Supergirl. Pregnancy now makes me feel like a more defined version of myself, as if someone has drawn around me in black felt-tip. I enjoy the way my body is changing: I like pausing in front of the mirror in our room while I get dressed, to see the curves thickening. But I also want to hold on to who I was before this pregnancy, as I know this is something I could lose, and my clothes matter, like clues to who I am apart from being a mother.

When I was a very young child, there often seemed to be pregnant women around my own mother, and I remember watching them, fascinated and sometimes horrified. A younger friend of hers, an art teacher who tied her hair on her head in a messy bun, usually wore small, loose denim shorts and moved with quick, neat movements, morphed into someone matronly, covering herself to her ankles in a long, stiff cotton dress covered in small printed flowers. And there were pictures of Princess Diana, pregnant, all over the newspapers my father read on Sundays. She had red flushed cheeks and wore something called a pie-crust collar. I worried about this, as if she might be turning into a pork pie. It was the early eighties, and pregnancy still looked like confinement, even to my childish eyes.

But then, one evening, I saw Neneh Cherry eight months pregnant, powerful and defiantly young, in a gold, cropped jacket and black Lycra rah-rah skirt, dancing on *Top of the Pops*. She made pregnancy look energetic, and something that turned her into a stronger version of herself, rather than hiding her. I was only twelve years old, but I knew that's how I wanted to be when I became pregnant. At twenty-four, when I was pregnant with Jimmy and maternity wear had arrived on the high street, all I could find were voluminous dresses decorated in fun polka dots, with pussy-cat bows placed, like fig leaves, on top of the bump. I didn't wear clothes like that, so instead I went to Dorothy Perkins and bought three clingy black dresses. They thankfully weren't the matronly Laura Ashley dresses of my mother's friends or, sadly, the lithe Lycra of Neneh Cherry, but by four months pregnant a size twelve would cling in most of the right places, and they only cost £10.99 each. I wore these three dresses through both my pregnancies with Jimmy and Dolly. And now, four months pregnant with my fifth child, aged forty-one, I buy myself a stretchy red dress which accentuates my body, and I feel good. Sexy, even.

I am never lonely when I am pregnant. That bunch of cells, a butterfly flicker, is now a baby with small fingers and identifiable limbs, moving between Pete and me when we lie in bed, separated from us only by skin and amniotic fluid. The green food I rejected two months ago is suddenly delicious and appealing. Dash and Evangeline might want to only eat pasta with butter, but Dolly is growing up, so that the green vegetables and whole pulses she pushed around her plate as a child are now completely acceptable to her. She likes standing in the kitchen with me, slicing red peppers and coriander as we talk about school, or throwing handfuls of fresh chilli over bright orange lentils. I'm conscientious, hoping my new appetite for whole foods will cancel out the white bread and sausage meat Dash and I consumed in the first few weeks. I crave lime juice and sharp tastes, but what I really, really want to eat is firelighters. I fantasize about their heady, white, petrol smell. But I can't eat firelighters, so instead I soak feta cheese in vinegar, and eat it, dripping, from a fork, alone in the kitchen, before the sleeping house wakes.

Pregnancy focuses me, switching on a timer counting down to when a baby – a whole new person bringing with it an entirely new personality – will be here and I will, for a while, need to stop work.

I am on a writing deadline. Pavel, our Czech au pair, plays with Dash and Evangeline after school, but when Dolly gets off the school bus outside our gate at 4 p.m. and comes to find me at my desk, she wants me to stop and drink tea with her. Words have been pouring out of me yet there are more I need to write. The clock is ticking, so I want to wring as much work from myself as I can before my time is up.

Even winter, a drawing down of the light, isn't enough to darken me. I feel productive and decisive; nothing scares or alarms me. I am a ship cutting quickly through the calm ocean around me, until I'm just over six months pregnant, when red spots appear in my pants.

My first miscarriage was ten months after Jimmy was born. It had started at thirteen weeks, with spots of blood that turned from dark brown to fresh bright red. In the hospital a young doctor rolled a condom down over a thick plastic probe and stuck it inside me, pressing upwards inside my womb, insistent and invasive, watching the screen in front of him.

'There is no heartbeat,' he said and withdrew his cold, hard instrument without making eye contact but offering me a D&C, 'to remove the matter left behind'. I didn't want this procedure, and drove home. Later I stood in the bathroom as blood ran down the inside of my legs, pooling on the lino floor. I caught the matter that the doctor had referred to in my hand, and I felt confused. It was not like a heavy period, and I did not want to flush it down the loo. It smelled raw and metallic, but it also was to have been a baby, a life, whose birthday should have been on 7 January. Afterwards I put it all in a tea towel and carried it outside. My sister was with me and we buried it under a tree because we had to do something.

The feeling was a twisted nerve of sharp pain, catching me when I moved in a certain direction, like whiplash. I could not look forward to the moment that might have been, the baby that might have been, but instead felt touched by an entirely new sort of loneliness, which pinched me when I wasn't looking. But I had Jimmy, so I blinked at him, and smiled when I opened my eyes as he patted his palms on my face, squeezing my grief back into myself and squashing it right down. It was the first time that motherhood had gone wrong for me. I'd cut into the raw liver and it had left blood on my hands.

At home I lie on my bed and think of my friend Alex. She has a daughter who is six, but it's taken another five failed pregnancies to get beyond that magical twelve-week mark with another child, and we are due within weeks of one another.

Alex carries her pregnancy carefully, cherishing the gift. She does not shove it into the bottom of her bag, as I have done, running between school gates so fast that often I see nothing but a blur.

'I'm aware of being pregnant every single moment of every single day. I'm never not thinking about it,' she has said to me.

I lie in bed and try to visualize the baby clinging on to me like a sea anemone, vivid and bright. I become intensely aware of each of its smallest movements and speak to the midwife regularly before I'm called in for another scan.

'Any rest you can get will help. It will help you, whatever happens,' she says, looking at notes. The scan is reassuring, the baby waving at me from its watery world. The blood had been dark brown, not red, and the midwife is optimistic and reassuring. As quickly as it starts, the spotting ends; the baby continues to move around inside me, somersaulting through the world we share together.

Back in the middle of the winter, when the days were endlessly dark, night and day bleaching into one another with little bright relief, I'd scanned long-term weather reports until I'd found one which said the summer would be long and sunny.

The report is right, because as the schools start breaking up, the sunshine days join together like a string of bright yellow beads. Dolly drags the paddling pool from the shed, tucking her skirt into her pants and standing barefoot in it, scrubbing last summer's dirt away with a brush. She and Evangeline fill the cubes of an ice tray with orange squash to freeze, and she helps Dash pull a bench out on to the lawn to set up an ice-cream stand for Evangeline's dolls. Everyone is barefoot, all the time, walking dried grass through the house.

Dash wears no clothes at all, only his skin of sunshine. Heat hangs around the house, so that we sleep with every bedroom window flung open, and my hair is always damp.

Sometimes, in those last few days of pregnancy, when I lie still in bed, feeling the baby moving inside me, a sharp nudge of memory points me back to the time Jimmy was a newborn baby. He was almost as small as this one, all curled up, something that hardly seems possible given how he looks now, the speed at which he has grown from that baby into a child into almost-a-guy, almost-a-bloke, with long legs, long calves ending in huge shoes and trousers slung low on his hips.

He spends more and more time separate from family life. I miss him, but since I've always encouraged him to spend time outdoors, I'm also thrilled to find he is spending less time over a laptop, lost on social media, but out instead, camping with his mates, every weekend! I believe everything he tells me because I love hearing tales of how they fell asleep listening to owls, or made a tent from a piece of tarpaulin which held up, even as a storm crackled around them. I'm delighted that he knew how to light a fire using wet wood the next morning, quietly smug that all those painfully uncomfortable camping trips I took him and Dolly on when they were small have fed into his teenage life. I boast about it to Pete. 'I don't think I've ever seen a teenager who lives outdoors or loves the natural world as much as Jimmy. As his mother it's so . . . gratifying,' I gush, not really caring how smug I sound.

I don't see anything of his new life because it's always happening somewhere else. When he comes home from school and goes straight upstairs to his room, I think it's just because he's avoiding the unbelievable noise of the younger kids in the kitchen. When he looks a bit blurry, I imagine it's just because he's tired from all those camping trips.

But even if you stare very hard at a plant like a tulip or a lily that opens quickly if you leave it in a warm kitchen, you never see it moving and completely changing in front of you, and it was the same with Jimmy. Because when I was fussing in the hospital with scans at the end of my pregnancy, worrying over the hoofbeats of the tiny baby's heart, Jimmy had been getting stoned out camping, then stoned at school and then stoned on the school bus. I had my eye on the wrong child, all the time.

This pregnancy doesn't end as it did in my fantasies. Pete did eventually go out to buy the recliners I wanted, but the only people lying on them calling for drinks were Dash and Evangeline, jelly beans in new swimsuits. After that difficult, confusing meeting with the headmistress, I spent most of the last days of being pregnant hiding behind the bins at the back of the house – the only place the kids won't look to find me – phone glued to my head, gulping down fraught conversations with Pete and different school officials about what happens next to my grown-up boy. How do we punish? Should we punish, even? Should he see a therapist? How do we ground him? What about exclusion? Or should we in fact be giving him more attention? I wanted the end of pregnancy to be soothing, but instead my emotions are like snooker balls, cracking off one another with the slightest provocation as I try to figure my way through this new maze. I consider taking up smoking again, then remember I can't.

For the first time as a mother, I feel that the vast, furious adolescent energy hanging around Jimmy, moving with him from bedroom to kitchen, is there just to break the bonds that have bound us so tightly, so closely, all the way through childhood, until now. I do not feel I have much agency in this; something way bigger than I am, and bigger than I am as his mother, is compelling us further and further apart, once magnets, now repelled.

2

Birthing Waters

At forty weeks my womb and my back and my thighs ache. I urgently want to be not pregnant now but even having that thought makes me feel a pinch of remorse because I'm supposed to be enjoying every single moment of this. Other women tell me all the time that, when it's gone, I'll miss it. So I cling on, like a passenger grasping the edge of the seat in an aeroplane when turbulence throws it around the sky.

I am sheared off from the rest of the world, far more separated from my life as a mother of four and a wife than I've ever been before. The only real allegiance I feel is to other pregnant women. When I pass two women in the street who must both be in their third trimester, I have to resist the urge to follow them, like a cow looking for its herd.

'Maybe the point of labour is to wake you up to what motherhood can be like,' Alex said when we met,

when we were both close to the end of our pregnancies, at her house. She put her hand on her bump, stroking it affectionately, like a much-loved pet. 'This bit of
pregnancy is tiring, but I think I'll miss this bump, this
sense of the baby being inside me, so close.'

I want her composure. My bump doesn't feel like a
pet, but an alien I urgently want to expel from my personal space. She stands up, raising her arms above her
head so that a clutch of silver bracelets rattles down her
arms as she stretches out the extraordinary bends of
her body, like a cobra that swallowed a goat.

'Nobody really tells you what this bit is like, or how
brutal just getting to here can be. All those miscarriages
I went through, all that blood and loss, just to get to this
point, and it's not even started,' she says, shaking her
thick blonde ponytail over her shoulders. She is ripe,
every part of her thick and luxurious, her hair like a
rope, her body swollen but her lips and her cheeks and
wrists slightly thickened, too. 'Nobody talks about how
much motherhood hurts. And nobody really tells you
how fundamentally it changes you.' She smiles at me
suddenly. 'Becoming a mother has been harder and
darker than I could ever have dreamed. But also wonderful. It's more wonderful and extraordinary and
strange than I could have imagined. And this point
where we are now, here' – she motions to our huge
bellies – 'this is not the end. Even if you might want
pregnancy to be over, labour is just the start.'

Late at night, when the rest of the house sleeps, I
stop worrying about Jimmy for a bit and I think of this
start that Alex is referring to. I watch a birth video on
YouTube which tells me to think of myself as a cervix,

stretching. This isn't that difficult. I am hot, swollen, throbbing with richest fertility. I am the living embodiment of sex, pure sex, when it's the purest primal and most animal function.

The hours and days before a baby arrives, before the 'due date', are both completely rooted in the daily mundane – since I can no longer fantasize about running away, because I can't run and who would have me, anyway, at forty weeks? – and also utterly surreal. Life has not just paused, but been yanked to a complete standstill. Every day tastes of raspberry-leaf tea and smells of clary sage.

'Haven't you had it yet?' people say, so that I have to resist the urge to growl: No, I'm waiting, in fact I'm holding on just to piss you, in particular, off.

Waiting for pregnancy to draw to its huge, terrifying conclusion is like standing on the edge of a wilderness, with all your belongings and all your longings strapped into a backpack, wondering who you might have become when you have crossed through this new land and returned home. It's like the ultimate Bear Hunt. You can't go over it and you can't go under it, so you have to go through it. For the first time, I feel alone even when I'm surrounded by Pete and the children. I cannot tell them how lonely this is. I must not show them that I am fearful, now, of stepping out on to the brink between life and death.

And in those last days, as I stand contemplating the wilderness, trying to organize my backpack as best I can, I keep thinking of a neat, well-organized couple I've seen on the back of a leaflet I picked up in the bank. It was a leaflet about financial planning before having a baby, and lay beside other leaflets about more things that can take you close to financial ruin if not given some serious thought: bereavement, retirement, moving house, redundancy. 'It's never too soon to start planning ahead,' it says, over a picture of a woman with a bright white smile, beaming at a three-wheel buggy, with a man whose main defining features are that his shirt is tucked into his trousers and his smile is as bright as the woman's.

I want to know if that woman and I will tackle the wildness of new motherhood in the same way? Even though I have done childbirth four times before, I feel as though I'm walking on to land I've never crossed, with no map and no water, probably wearing the wrong sort of shoes. In fact, probably wearing no shoes at all. I am highly likely to survive childbirth, but I will be changed by it, too. I will pass through the wilderness, but things will be different afterwards. It is, if not scary, at least very unsettling.

Finally, I am counting the hours. Time is like a cartoon presence in the room with me. Minutes and moments float past like thought bubbles drawn with a thick black-tipped pen. Will it be this minute? Or that moment? This afternoon? This evening?

Dash and Evangeline run up and down the upstairs corridor, shrieking. Later, when I pin them to the bed, tucking their sheets around them to try to make them submit to the night, they start shrieking again. Maybe our baby will be here tomorrow! Maybe our baby will have come when we wake up and we can cuddle it! I flop down on the bed beside them and think of labouring in my bedroom, at the end of the corridor, with the rest of the house around me. I can almost remember what my labour screams are like and I am certain they would traumatize all my children. They would make the house sound as if I was either being murdered or mustering my powers to horribly murder someone else.

This isn't something I want and, anyway, I like hospitals. They don't scare me; even though during my life many frightening things have happened in hospital to people I really love, I still think of them as wonderful safe places where babies come from.

I want to fold myself into the clean white envelope of hospital, with the safety of the doctors and oxygen all around. I want a drug-free labour, but I also want to be close to safety, and for me that means hospital, however much I love giving birth. Also, there's a pile of dirty laundry in our bedroom and a mark on the wall where the damp comes through and I don't want to be distracted by these when I'm having the baby. I don't want the spiritual business of labour to be interrupted by housework.

I tuck the sheets closer around Evangeline, her blonde hair splayed out on the pillow around her, and then try to pin down Dash, who squirms to get back on to the floor and far away from sleep, right back to his train tracks.

'Look, Dash, lie with me and see if you can see this baby moving,' I coo into his ear, trying to do anything to force him to settle down, so that I can, too. Dash pulls the duvet off, unlodging a clatter of wooden trains hidden on his bedclothes, and tries to throw himself on top of me.

'My baby here?' he shrieks. I grab him, pinning him down, close to violence, while burying my face in the sweet, soft reassurance of his neck, which smells of very slightly grubby pyjamas and buttery toast, and while I purr at him, inside I'm screaming: Dear God make this end.

It's dark when I wake up, and even though I know what to expect, I'm still shocked by what my body is doing. It has a power that's separate from me, Clover, that woman who worries and cooks and drives the children about and holds them tight. I have no agency in this. My body will do exactly what needs to be done almost without me being present. Lying still in the dawn as light creeps around me, I feel so alone that it's as if I am the last person alive in the world.

And the wetness all around me in the sheet isn't like the warm memory of relief that peeing in my pants could feel like when I was a small girl. It doesn't feel like I've wet the bed, although the sheets are soaked. For a moment I lie still, breathing shallowly, before the new world which I know I'm about to step into is made real.

I sling my legs over the edge of the bed, wriggling my toes and staring out into the pale blue morning light with the ancient line of the Ridgeway rising beyond the black barn outside our house. The red figures of the digital clock beside my bed glow like an angry insect and it is 4 a.m. On normal days it's difficult to see the changes happening in my life. I walk onwards and it's only when I look back at the longer picture that it is clear life has shifted in the most profound and startling way. The nightmares I dreaded have become real. The unthinkable and unbearable has been thought and borne. Beloved women have died. But also, precious babies have been born, bonds of friendship formed and broken and re-formed again, kitchens painted bright pink and then papered over with vivid flowers a little later. I have found delight all around me, even in the dark. Beds have been made up with new fresh sheets and I have slept in them. I have dreamed of a life I wanted and then gone forward to create and live it. All this has happened in the everyday without me really noticing. But the moment before birth is quite different, as if it's been crystallized: it's the moment that I can touch, when I can say, truly, yes, this life is happening to me right now. It is not existing in the past, lamented, or there in the future, longed for, but right here, a hot spark in my hand in the morning light.

It is one of the warmest weeks of the year, and yet dense white mist coats every strand and leaf of the land outside, pressing right up against the house, smothering into the window. The hospital in Oxford is half an hour from our home and, as I remember this, I feel a tightening register from a deep place of caution inside me. I breathe and breathe, pushing my top lip out as if I'm playing a flute. Pete wakes up beside me, putting his hand on my back, his voice calling me darling, darling. I walk around the room, and for the first time in weeks my movements are small and precise, rather than huge, lumbering, heavy. My breath is shallow, and a tuning fork is humming inside me like the feeling I used to get after I'd taken ecstasy and was waiting to feel high and wild and other.

I call the hospital. The midwife is relaxed and she asks me what the pain feels like. 'Just very gentle, a tightening. The first contraction was ten minutes ago and there was another just then,' I say, a spy quickly relaying vital information from another world. There's a shuffling and then a sound of screaming in the background, the soundtrack to a midwife's professional life. She tells me to lie down for a little longer, and to stay at home until the contractions are moving faster.

'This is my fifth child,' I say, because suddenly my heart is racing, as if the high is about to really kick in. 'Are you sure? I'm half an hour away in a car. I don't think there's going to be much hanging around.'

Pete motions for me to put the phone down. 'No, Clover, we need to go now,' he says, pulling on his shirt. 'We need to go right now,' he repeats quickly, going to wake Pavel to warn him, for when the children wake up later.

The early-morning dampness clings to us, seeping into the car as we leave the house. It is 4.15 a.m., so there are few other cars on the road with us. Pete drives fast into the clouds of mist and for the first time I am really frightened. It feels as though we're heading into a wall. The tightening and pain is suddenly happening too quickly. I watch the clock on the dashboard and there's less than four minutes between each contraction. Pete says we'll be fine and we'll get there really soon, but his voice sounds so distant to me, and it's irritating. I'm moving away from him and over into the outer reaches where this car and the road and the mist are unimportant, and perhaps don't really exist.

My body has started making a noise too, from deep in my chest, a low moaning, as I brace myself against the hard plastic of the dashboard to try and push the pain away from me. When we come to the string of roundabouts before the city, Pete doesn't stop, driving as though we're in a car chase. I don't want to notice this. It means he's scared, or he's worried that we might not make it in time and that the baby will be born on the car seat. I don't want the baby's first view to be the empty Costa cups rattling around on the floor of Pete's car and I don't want to have to lie down on tarmac to have the baby, either.

The contractions are hard and fast by the time we're in the city centre and I get out of the car directly in front of the special entrance to the Women's Centre. Fluid runs down my legs, soaking the front of my nightdress, splashing on the concrete, and startling a man in an electric-blue tracksuit having a quiet cigarette outside the building. When the electric doors don't respond to me, remaining shut tight, I behave like a possessed woman in a zombie movie, slapping both palms flat on to the door, trying to get in, howling with pain. I have a sense of the man, even more horrified than me, dancing around and yanking the doors open with both hands, but I don't look at his face as all of the world is whirring away from me and my head and my body are shattering into pieces, as a midwife takes my arm, into an elevator, and up, up, up into the sky, into the birthing unit on the top floor of the hospital.

My head is a cracked enamel sieve with wet sand pouring through it. Sand is rushing through my ears and running down my back. It's scratching under my fingernails and inside my eyelids. I want to escape this sand as that big wave approaches. It's not here yet but I know it is coming.

I feel burning, too, so that my shoulders tense up as they do when sun-hot skin slaps into salt water. Everything is light and there's movement all around me and I feel the waters are rushing up to meet my out-stretched hands.

Don't touch me. Don't touch any part of me.

Let me feel every part of myself. Let me exist just inside me. I'm scared to turn outwards and look at the woman beside me. She's dressed in navy blue with big bulbous white shoes, bouncing up to my vision sud-denly when I want them and her and everything in this room to be far away.

'Clover, I'm going to be back in a few moments, I need to get another monitor.' It's as if she's speaking to me through a megaphone and whispering at the same time and I reach out to grab her, afraid she will suddenly vanish, because now I violently don't want her to go.

'I won't be long, a few moments. You are doing really well.' She glances up to Pete who is beside me, I'm sure he is, and something silent passes between them.

They talk, and she is gone for a moment, but back quickly. I am the third person in the room and their voices are very far away while also right inside my ear.

'She's doing well.'

'She'll be fine, she's very strong. And brave. She's exceptionally strong.' That must be Pete speaking, I think.

'They're coming every few seconds now. This will be hurting. She's feeling big contractions.'

I can sense him watching me. Sometimes he reaches out when I need him. Then he presses the skin at the bottom of my back as I lean into him, because it feels as if my body will actually explode. And now another part of me I didn't know existed until this moment comes alive, like a viper in a corked jar. It's lashing and hissing and desperate to get out, to erupt like a whole cask of snakes, a Medusa presence.

The lightness around me shatters and the wave rushes up to me and bursts on top of me so that a sound like nothing I've heard before comes from me. I'm screaming and grasping at my body, trying to rip this sand out of me. The skin around my legs and between my legs is on fire, burning with a pain that's going to rip my body right in half.

I reach down and press at the pain that's going to rip through my clitoris, my vulva, the pain that is going to destroy, and somehow is also part of, my cervix. I've never felt anything so hard in my body as this feeling now, of the baby coming out of me. I can't breathe my way through this so instead I scream and I scream and I scream and I touch myself, pressing my forefinger and middle finger hard against my clitoris. Nobody tells you this but it is true: your clitoris has the highest number of nerve endings in your whole body. It's why sex feels good. Press hard on it in labour and you might be a little distracted from the pain ripping through you. My body feels like iron now as the pain presses down on me, something like hot steel moving in bands inside me, expanding. Pressing my clitoris changes the feeling though. The hurt doesn't disappear, but it does transform. Instead of being magnified between my legs, it ripples away from me and just as being fucked so hard it hurts can feel good, this pain becomes something I recognize as clearly as I know myself.

I lean forward and squat down and Medusa returns as a roar, because something primal and then absolutely human comes from me, the baby, the new person, rushing through my body, fire burning through my vulva as my world shatters and opens all around me. I'm soaring, free, completely in the room and in no way part of it at all. I'm eternal but I'm here as I am born into another place that's nowhere I've ever been before. It's the most terrifying space of my life and it's home, home, home. It's everything; it's ecstasy and terror as I feel the baby's head between my legs, the wave of sand and water, of adrenalin and fear and relief and horror becoming a new life and he's here, we're swimming through the light and ancient new waters together. He's here. He's in the room.

In that moment that he arrives, the baby is pure and somehow very, very old. It's as if he has taken a huge gulp of life. He's white and blue and bloody with tiny shoulders, tiny bottom and little clawing arms uncurling. They are the exact, strange, greasy blue of the umbilical cord that ties him on to me, feeling wet and startling between my legs. One hour before I was sitting on my bed at home. One hour later I'm ecstatic and gasping, yanking huge breaths of air inside me as a new human being is passed across to Pete. Everything that he is, is there in the room. He is not a blank slate but a fully formed adult, less baby than he will be for a long time. It's as if babyhood, the babyhood we understand from blue and pink greeting cards, is something that the world will bestow on to him.

I am squatting when he is born, and he arrives so fast that the midwives have to quickly throw a piece of paper towelling on to the ground beneath my legs to stop the splatter of liquid on the floor as his head started crowning. Now I pull myself on to the bed, pushing away from me the memory of the hot, burning feeling of his body coming out of mine. The pain of the baby arriving is a mythical pain that almost has no space in my mind. It's not the blunt stupidity of the pain of stubbing my toe, or the shrieking, metallic pain of slicing into my finger with a sharp knife when cooking. The feeling of childbirth is a sensation beyond this, entirely of its own. In that moment of the birth I am not in the room, or in this city, or in a hospital, but at the far end of a telescope that pointed inwards to my brain and deep inside me.

I would do anything to go back to that moment when my children are arriving. Going through labour a second or third or fifth time has all of the intensity of the first time. Experience does not dull it; labour still scares me and I think that's right because it should be a scary thing. The arrival of a new life is the most epic thing I can imagine doing on an otherwise unremarkable Thursday evening or Sunday morning. A friend who had an epidural as her contractions started told me she watched *Britain's Got Talent* and then *EastEnders* throughout her labour, and slept a bit, until the midwife told her it was time to push. That's how she wanted to do it, but I cannot help feeling she missed the most important moment of her life.

After the violence of labour, holding the baby in my arms while gulping in his sweet perfect beauty makes me gasp yes and yes and yes again, because the sense of rightness is absolute. It is like the feeling of sex when something much bigger, stronger than you takes over and you lose all parts of yourself. Held skin on skin, my contact with the baby I have just birthed is the most perfect union I will ever experience. Time is absent from where we are, but I know we lie like that together for a while, the midwife silently moving in and out of the room, filling in papers. I am holding the baby, and Pete is holding me and the baby, and I feel as though I have given him every part of myself. We are laughing, gasping, flooded with loving. We are everything I have ever dreamed we could be, and Pete is grinning, euphoric.

'I love you, I love you, I love you, hello, you, I love you,' he says, half laughing and half crying, and the energy dazzles. It's the best, brightest, rightest feeling in the world.

My body, though, feels blubbery, smeared with bloody fluid, suddenly emptied. More stuff pours from me and so I pass the warm, slippery baby to Pete and a blanket is wrapped around him, a tiny white woollen hat slipped on his head. It's not all over for me, because the placenta has to be delivered.

And that delivery of the placenta really, really hurts. My babies have all been born while I was standing up, or crouching, or leaning up against a hospital bed, rocking, moaning, screaming, but always on two feet. That way, gravity is in my favour, and by stretching I can move the baby downwards. But each of my five placentas has been delivered on my back, legs apart, the way most (almost certainly male) filmmakers represent childbirth. The midwife teases the placenta out, because although it contains no bones or precious brain like the baby, it still has to be born. It has been the invisible guardian angel, securing the baby to the edge of the uterus and filtering goodness to him, while receiving his waste back into my blood. It's deep magic, the dark red curtain between life and death which must stay in place because if it had come away during pregnancy the baby would have died. Now it looks like a colossal piece of dark red liver, quivering in a bright metal dish. The midwife holds it up, admiring, and while I look away, a part of me, like a wild animal, also wants to eat it.

And even after the placenta has been delivered, there's more war surgery to be done: put your legs up in hooks and let us stitch through your fanny now. It is at least a chance to get going on the gas and air again. I drift far, far away to a childhood memory of being beside a lake with my sister. In my dreams I'm holding the bridle of my pony, the delicious, druggy, swirling delirium of that dream only broken by a metallic rattling sound I think is the pony shaking its bridle, but is in fact the sound of the nurse's medical instruments hitting the metal trolley as she does her work. I hear her voice saying she's almost done, but I take another massive draught and think I'll tell her to take as long as she possibly can.

When I return to the room, the baby is handed back to me, wrapped in a little white sheet. A new baby is very serious. This one lies in my arms, and stares, with eyes like flints. I feel a relieved sense of recognition, of course – it was you all the time – but the baby seems to be considering the choice he has made, trying to work me out and decide if he really wants to stay. He peers cautiously out into the world, as if it's by no means a foregone conclusion.

'Would you like to stay?' says a midwife, leaning her head around the door. I have been moved from the birthing room into a little single room at the side of the midwifery unit, at the top of the hospital. With the baby wrapped in a blanket and pressed into a plastic cot, a perfect little chrysalis on a leaf, I have stood under a shower, warm water running down my warrior's body, blood straight from the battlefield pouring out of me, pooling at my feet and then swirling away, away. When I am clean, I hobble back across the room, ecstatic and completely spent, as I gaze at the baby in his cot.

At some point, someone delivered a cheese sandwich and a cup of tea to the table at the end of the bed, but I was sleeping. Pete has gone home to see the children and bring them back to the hospital. Unlike home, the white hospital room is neat and quiet, nothing out of place. Sunlight pours through the windows, which overlook the city. I love it here. It's the hospital where all my children have been born, and where my mother gave birth to me, too. She died when I was pregnant with Dash after a very long illness that separated her from me; staying a little longer in hospital is a way of feeling closer to her, too. I pad along linoleum floors, clutching my baby, just as she had done, and it helps me feel she is with me in some way after all.

Pete brings all the children to the hospital after school. I hear them in the corridor outside the room, a jumble of loud, sudden noises, Pete gently shushing them, because going into a midwifery unit can feel sacrosanct, a place where you should be reverent and quiet, so close to life and death.

I once read somewhere that when elder siblings arrive to see a new baby, the new mother should have the baby lying in the bedside cot, rather than in her arms, so that the elder children don't feel compromised, or usurped. When Dash pushes forward towards me, I stretch my arms out, preparing to brace myself for that way he flings himself at me, as if he's jumping off a wall. He throws trains at me, burying himself in me as if the baby is forgotten. But the girls are different. They are fragile and fluttering as little hummingbirds suddenly alighting on the baby's cot. Dolly has dressed Evangeline in a favourite white outfit that had been a bridesmaid's dress. I imagine her, at home, caring for Evangeline, fussing over her as she prepares her for this rite of passage. It might have mattered to her to exert some control over her little sister, too. She needed to be the *elder* sister as another baby arrives.

Now they coo and crane over the sleeping baby, absolutely feminine, hot with nurture, eyes shining, Evangeline's little hands reaching into the cot to stroke the baby as Dolly clucks at her: 'Be careful, Evangeline, remember he's brand new and doesn't know us yet,' her voice trembling. She carefully shows Evangeline how to reach into the cot, to lay him gently on the bed. Evangeline has an uncontrollable need to unwrap him and rewrap him in his little blanket, just like one of her dolls. We unfold him from the blanket so they can see his twig legs; Dolly strokes his tiny foot. Dash clambers around, standing on the bed, then pressing his fat hands on to the baby's face as if he wants to imprint himself into his younger brother as Dolly grabs him, chiding him and protecting the baby. Unperturbed, Dash holds a toy train directly in front of the baby's eyes. I think about stopping him then realize the baby had better get used to this.

'Train! Look train!' he says sternly, and starts running the wooden wheels over the baby's forehead before he suddenly sees his tiny fingers and minute nails. For a moment the urgency of showing his new brother the thing he loves most in the world vanishes as Dash slips his palm underneath the baby's. 'Hands! Hands!' he says, delighted by what he, and nobody else, has found.

Jimmy bobs around by the door, catches my eye, smiling quickly as I reach out my hand to him, because I want to pull him tight into this new family group too.

He lifts his hand, waves at me from the far side of the room. This is supposed to be a time of happiness, the introduction of the new baby into the family, and at this moment I want to put what's happened in the last few days into the past, to stop it spilling into this room.

'He's sweet, Mum. Really sweet,' Jimmy says; then he reaches up, unrolling all six feet of himself, his long arms almost touching the ceiling. He's massive; I can never get over how massive he is.

When I was pregnant with Dash, I read that a child – a person – is most pleasing to his or her mother on the first day of life, as a newborn baby. This was in a book of birth stories, but something about it shocked me, casting a bleach of disappointment over my sense of what lay ahead. I'd already had three children by that point: Jimmy and Dolly were thirteen and ten, and Evangeline had grown out of babyhood and was toddling, so I knew, very clearly, that motherhood was a way of life that played out lows just as much as highs; I'd also experienced the inimitable and absolutely singular joy of holding a new baby in my arms, but I didn't want to think that this was the peak.

Although the idea troubled me, and still does, I also know that, when I look back at the first two weeks of each of my five children's lives, I was probably happier and more fulfilled as a mother during this time than at any other. Those ten weeks when my perfect five were a couple of weeks old each are the purest, happiest times of my life. Of course they are exhausting, vulnerable times, too, filled with the physical challenges of having just given birth, which means managing the disposal of huge quantities of bloody liquid that pours out of me for anything up to three months after a birth, and the knife-sharp pain of teaching a new baby to latch on to cracked, bleeding nipples: a unique agony. But those first two weeks are also like magic, since mothering in its most intense, consuming, tender sense is all that occupies the days. The demands of the world are away.

We call him Lester. Just before he was born, a friend who also has a grown-up son called Lester had posted on Facebook a black and white photograph of Lester Piggott as a teenage jockey. In the photograph he has a look of absolutely clear determination and purpose, so much so that it almost makes me cry looking at him. He looks brave and clever, too. I ask my friend if he minds if we copy the name, and he is pleased. It's a good name, he says. A strong name. Pete and I try the name out together as we hold our son. It feels a little strange, at first, bestowing something that sounds formal and grown up on this little baby, but by the time we leave hospital with Lester, that's who he is. We've both learned, from previous babies, not to ask anyone else for their opinion ('*Dash*? Really? *Dash*?'), but instead to use the name as if that's what it's always been.

I feel completely changed as I walk back into the house and into the kitchen, with Lester like a tiny grub on my shoulder. Everything seems to shimmer with a special sort of light that's different from the slow heaviness of my last days of pregnancy. Colours seem brighter, the house sweeter, with tiny babygros Evangeline takes for her dolls hanging on the washing line. There are white roses from my father and stepmother, a yellow bunch of roses from someone I work with. Cards cover every surface. Someone has sent a blue fluffy monkey. It's cute, but I also want to surround this baby with serious things, something strong and ancient and intensely physical. I won't read them, but I want the Complete Works of Shakespeare and the Bible on my bedside table.

I'm not aware of it immediately and won't truly recognize it for some time, but in those first few hours, few days, with a new baby, a quiet madness settles around me. Often it's as comforting as the smell of lavender essence I sprinkle in my bath, or the sweetness of the feeling of the top of Lester's head. If you could lift me out of my day now and drop me back into any other I've lived before, I'd go back there, to the moments when all my babies were brand new. The intoxicating gold of Lester's little head is the definition of happy to me now. And with it, I think I am a new person, someone who can make the things I have got wrong as a mother all better and right. This special madness that comes to me after birth is soft, and I snuggle down into it; it lulls me into believing I can keep the imprint of newness and optimism with me for ever. Lester is perfect, his tiny pink lips pursed, eyes pressed shut, folded into a white waffle blanket in my arms. The world starts again when a baby is born, like a felt rubber across a blackboard wiping the mess and marks away.

This is ecstasy pumping gently through me; it's not too shrill and not so obvious that I'm high, but I am, I later realize, much later, unquestionably in an altered state of consciousness. It might take me in several directions. It's a very strong drug.

3

Milky Days and Skin Gloves

There are new relationships to navigate now that we have become seven in the house. All of us have moved in relation to one another, like chess pieces. Evangeline needs Pete more, demanding his attention, accompanying him on every shopping trip for nappies and cotton wool, holding his hand as he walks through the house. Dash finds his way into our bedroom at every chance, staring at me intently as I try to tease my huge, dark red nipples into the impossibly tiny cavity of Lester's lighter pink mouth. Dolly is busy, organizing clean little sheets for the Moses basket beside our bed, unpeeling the cabbage leaves I've put into the freezer. It's not an old wives' tale and they really are the only real relief I can find for my throbbing, engorged breasts.

'Oh Mum, poor you, that looks agony,' she says, trying not to grimace as I wince at the pain of feeding. She shoos Dash out of my room with a promise to make train tracks with him in the kitchen, growing more maternal and capable by the moment.

How Jimmy and I fit together in this new family puzzle is less clear. I do not like holding on to my anger. I don't have it in me to be perpetually cross and distant, and anyway I struggle to feel anger or, really, manifest any kind of authority while holding Lester in my arms. I am completely at a loss as to how to make him talk to me, to look at me, or even to be in the same room as me. I do not feel I know how to mother my teenage boy.

Lester, meanwhile, has come from another place, both fluid and air-filled, bringing a sort of enchantment with him. My father holds him as though he's a little hand grenade, but he also says to me: 'Oh Clove, oh Clove, well done, you, well done, my darling.'

Every woman who comes to the house – my sisters, my stepmother, girlfriends – wants to hold him, staring into his face to soften and coo, breathing in the top of his head as if he's a warm loaf of freshly made bread. Then they want to hand him carefully back.

Kathryn arrives to kiss him a few days after I get home. She melts, almost gurgling with desire, and walks around the kitchen, snuggling him against her chest, whispering and clucking at him. We had stepped around one another after I'd told her I was expecting. I didn't cajole for a date, as I might have done before, not wanting to thrust the fact of my pregnancy into her face when it was the only thing she wanted. Now, though, the new baby brings us back together. I am deeply relieved when she arrives, one evening, just as I am struggling to placate Dash and persuade him to leave his toys and have a bath, as Lester mews on my shoulder, in need of yet another feed. Kathryn swoops in, grappling with Dash as if carrying a dolphin upstairs, plopping him into the bath and turning it all into a game.

'Hmmm, it's a handful, isn't it,' she says, when she re-emerges downstairs, looking thrashed. 'Almost makes me relieved I've just got one. Almost.'

For a while I feel clever and very strong. For once, my role as a mother is something admired, not the flavour of day-to-day mothering I know from the slog of the school gates, or the daily grind of pleading with the children to make them engage with their homework, pasta, baths and pyjamas.

The drama of the birth remains close to us, and I feel it in the pain of my stitches. Lester is still so small he could fit back into my squashy and deflated stomach, but I know that this newborn stage will retreat into the past very quickly. I feel untethered from the rest of the family and even what's going on in the house. Lester alone is under my emotional magnifying glass. Lying on our bed as Pete cooks supper for the children downstairs, I silently watch Lester as he startles in the Moro reflex, his hands suddenly stiff, when a slamming door or shriek from one of the other children surprises him. He lies with one arm pulled back, the other outstretched, like a miniature archer, or swipes the air, moving his head slowly, an ancient tortoise. These are movements I know already, echoes of the way his body, shoulders or little heel and fingers pressed against me when he was still inside. With each day, those echoes of his internal positions grow weaker. They are his newborn characteristics, but in a few weeks he will have outgrown them; our shared physical memory of his internal world will have gone. When he feeds, I hold him close and he sighs and shudders.

Every morning, Evangeline runs into our bedroom as soon as she wakes up, her arms stuffed with babygros and tiny vests. When he sleeps, she wants to wake him up to unwrap him so that he can play with her. 'Shall we change him?' I ask one morning as she sits on the bed beside me. She has her own plastic doll against her chest, her T-shirt pulled up, doing what I do. But her face brightens into a fast-shocked smile when I ask this.

'Change him? For something else? Like a pet?' she says, standing up quickly as her doll falls on to the floor, and she jumps up and down on the duvet. 'Can we really do that? Can we change him for a guinea pig?'

Alongside the intense joy of my feelings for my new baby is the serious business of teaching him how to feed, and relearning it myself. The physicality of teaching a newborn to latch on to a breast is abrasive: it makes me gasp. The pain of the milk 'coming in' to my breasts, on the third or fourth day after birth, is almost more shocking than labour itself, since it's slow, and constantly present, and doesn't end after a few hours, as labour does. Instead I must do normal things, like cook supper, or try to have a conversation – with the health visitor, one of my children, with Pete – as my breasts harden into massive, boiling rocks of pain, and my T-shirt displays two orbits of wetness.

My breasts no longer feel as if they are part of my body, but rather that they have been strapped on, like comedy body parts. However, there's absolutely nothing funny about them at all. Lester is the fifth baby I have breastfed but each time it hurts like hell to start with. I persist, though, because I know that, like all of the things that hurt me about being a mum, it will change and pass and just become a kind of pain I own while barely thinking about it. I also know the pain will bring pleasure, eventually. It will be worth the hurt.

But until then I scrunch my free hand into a fist when he tries to latch on, bracing myself, holding my breath, trying to forget that it feels like the tip of my nipple is being held in a metal clamp. My nipples are wounds that must be dressed and undressed many times a day. I smear lanolin on them and inside my breast pads, imagining the greasy sheep's wool that's brought me this magic ointment which stands between me and absolute torture. When Lester is screaming, ravenous and shaking with need, the only thing that will stop this fury in his tiny body, his tense limbs and rage, is to be attached to my wounds. Then he's no longer a sweet little limpet I want to cover with my kisses, but a vampire, devouring my bleeding, cracked nipples. A couple of times, when it's most difficult, I see smudges of red blood in the milk around his mouth when he finishes feeding.

'It's like being ripped to pieces by metal tongs then raped while it's happening,' was how Kathryn described her experience of the birth of her daughter, when I first met her in a feeding clinic, just after Evangeline was born. Her daughter was delivered using forceps after a fast labour that slowed to a standstill in the final stages, requiring invasive medical intervention.

There were many women in the clinic, most of them with pillows on their laps, some of them weeping quietly as they revealed their bleeding breasts, like stigmata, shocked into silence by what their baby was doing to them. The few husbands or partners standing by their wives looked stricken, as if being forced to watch extreme pornography or a horror film.

Kathryn looked like a painting in her bright red shirt with her thick, curly dark hair pulled messily back from her face. I sat down beside her, as her daughter lay asleep on her lap. She watched her with her shirt open and one breast exposed, as if they were completely alone.

Neither of us said anything and I waited, hoping Evangeline wouldn't wake up, until a woman with thick arms came and unwrapped her from her bundle and showed me how to move her small face to my breast in a quick, decisive movement that reminded me of trying to catch a wasp under a glass. I apologized to her for being there.

'I should know how to do this, she's my third baby,' I said, steeling myself to try the movement again.

'No reason to apologize at all. Breastfeeding can always be hard to start with,' she reassured me. 'It's certainly not the case that you can just sit there and do what comes naturally.' I tried it a few more times with the lady sitting beside me, and when I did it correctly, the way my baby's mouth felt on my nipple changed from a sharp, excruciating pinch to a satisfyingly strong tug. It was a relief and I would have been prepared to feed sitting up in a plastic chair all night if it meant the woman could stay by my side and show me how to do it.

Kathryn saw me relax, and immediately we started talking about our births, as if we were interviewing one another. I felt relieved by the way she talked completely openly about birth and death and even rape because the hushed things mothers usually talked about – let-down and breast pads and sleep routines – just felt like office admin in comparison to the emotional storms that becoming a mother again had unleashed inside me.

Kathryn told me that her daughter's delivery was so painful she had begged to be killed to make it end. 'And I cried for an hour almost without stopping,' she said. 'It still plays in my head all the time, the birth, if I don't force myself to think of something else. I feel as if something complicated but precious has been taken away from me, like losing my virginity.'

We sat in silence after that. I wasn't sure I should tell her that giving birth had terrified me and that I had made noises and done things that I didn't really like to remember, but also that it had been the most profound experience of my life. Instead I said that 'complicated and precious' was a good description of what being a new mother felt like. Later, I discovered that one of the reasons Kathryn wanted another baby so badly was to experience a completely different birth. 'I wanted to reclaim it, after everything that happened.'

When I finish feeding Lester, I walk around the house with one of my breasts exposed, like a sliced grapefruit. I don't notice it, even when Jimmy walks into the kitchen, then leaves quickly, looking down. I only realize later, when I'm standing by the cooker, stirring onions, and I feel something warm and wet at my feet, as if the cat has left the insides of a small animal there for me to find. It's milk, pouring out of me and dribbling down my bare feet. I am a blur. I cannot see myself any more.

Maybe this is because as I retreat into a separate world with Lester, dictated by his need to be fed and soothed and fed again, I am gradually becoming an addict. No one warns you what the pain of labour is really like, but no one tells you about this feeling, either, because once the bleeding, throbbing agony of my breasts settles, and both Lester and I have learned or remembered what a good latch feels like, breastfeeding is a flood of hormones like pure liquid heaven running through me. It's a fix. Exhaustion, having walked across the battlefield of labour, and oxytocin, the new-baby hormone, are a strong combination. There are moments, alone with Lester as he clamps his tiny mouth around my nipple, when I imagine this is what injecting myself with heroin might feel like. It's something like a distant bliss flooding through my veins, my ego obliterated.

I yearn for him. In those first few days and weeks, I don't want anything else. I want to see his face, and hear his name, and smell him and touch him all the time. It's like being in love, the consuming physical passion and romance I've felt for men I have loved and wanted to devour or possess. It's so physical, this passion.

I am also completely fucked.

'Baby brain!' exclaims the man at the supermarket checkout, laughing, when I put a trolley of shopping through the till before realizing I've left my purse somewhere else – on the kitchen table, or by my bed, or in the bag I thought I wouldn't need when I left the house.

At the same time Lester, who is strapped to me in a baby carrier, starts wriggling, waking from a sleep. I feel him uncurling, pressing his back against the carrier, nuzzling around looking for my nipple. My breasts feel heavy as udders as I start dancing gently on the spot to distract him as wetness soaks through my T-shirt.

The man is kind. 'Don't worry! It happens to ladies a lot with young babies, you're not the first!' He laughs again, making every one of his sentences end in an exclamation mark, perhaps to make the humiliation of being part of this stupid, addled club less intense. 'Shall I pack it up for you anyway and keep it by the side, if you want to come back later, once you've sorted the little one out?'

I nod and retreat from the store, tears brimming in my eyes. I am overwhelmed by a crashing sense of failure. Getting out of the house to the supermarket, dashing around while throwing courgettes and pasta and a chicken into the trolley had made me sweat, but I had thought I'd managed it. I thought I was behaving like a good mother, running our house efficiently, providing for hungry children who would soon be home from school, while also nursing a newborn baby. I try to tell myself that forgetting my purse is not a major test of character, but what I feel is stupid, vacant, inefficient, chasing my tail, getting nowhere.

The man in the queue behind me has been scrolling through his phone but stops to check on what the hold-up is. At a neighbouring till, another mother, better organized, calmer, cleaner, probably *nicer* than me, is chatting to her toddler in the trolley as she packs yogurts and bags of apples and oranges into a canvas carrier. She has a shopping list in one hand, and a neat biro line through everything on the list.

In the car I release Lester from the buckles and straps that hold him against me, pushing the seat back to fit his tiny body, juddering with hunger and his need for comfort, between me and the steering wheel. I grip the wheel as he latches on, and a thin, sour smell of spilt milk surrounds me; the front of my T-shirt is sodden in two big, milky rings. No man has ever been told he has a baby brain, I think, as Lester sucks and nestles and sighs, a dribble of my milk, sweet and white, trickling gently from his mouth.

I am pressed up close against Lester but I see Jimmy less and less. In the last days of term, he moves from the school bus to his room in one swift, silent movement. Even when we are in the same room, it's like I am holding on to his shadow as he walks away from me. The trouble he has got himself into has begun to feel like my fault, too. I should have been holding him closer. I should have been paying attention.

The drugs policy at his school means he will have to move, but even having a conversation with Pete about this is difficult, as there's little space to think, let alone talk and make clear plans. We try, late at night, when I'm feeding Lester, or quickly, on the phone, while Pete's at work, but there are no conclusions and really this trouble is mine to deal with. The school has cancelled Jimmy's work experience, scheduled for the end of term. He had been looking forward to it: two weeks working in a studio in east London with a friend who is a sculptor. When I call my friend to apologize he doesn't sound surprised, or shocked. 'Oh, he's a teen-ager so of course he's going to be smoking weed,' he said vaguely, as if he had his eye on something else as he was talking to me. He offered to have Jimmy another time, later in the year. 'And what can he learn from this? Take drugs while you are listening to music or on the dance floor, I suppose. Just don't take drugs at school.'

It is the first time I feel really annoyed with the school: surely equipping him with life skills is exactly what Jimmy needs now, not shutting up for two weeks in isolation?

I try not to communicate my sense of irritation at this decision by the school to Jimmy, and to Dolly and the younger children; I have to appear calm. I do not want them to know about it. I am in limbo, until a call, a few days after Lester's birth, with a social worker specializing in educational outreach, allotted to me by the school to try and work out what happens next to Jimmy.

'In one sense, it's lucky we're not talking about a criminal charge, Miss Stroud,' he says, and the serious, enclosed silence enveloping his voice makes me think he's in an office, an adult workspace that's separate from the rest of his life. I can't remember what that feels like. There's no sound of slammed doors, or small feet thundering on stairs, or small fists pounding on the closed bathroom door.

My bedroom floor is covered by a trail of Evangeline's dolls' clothes, two hairdryers tangled together that Dolly had given up on, some small metal cars in a neat line and a packet of newborn nappies that's exploded among them like leaflets strewn everywhere. Wet towels sit on the rug reproachfully and there's a mounting pile of washing in the corner by the door. I am naked from the waist upwards, sitting on the edge of my bed on a towel that covers the patch of blood where the sanitary towel has failed to hold more of the blood that still seeps out of me, especially when I stand up.

Outside the window, Dash's voice rises in a crescendo and then falls as he runs backwards and forwards through a sprinkler on the lawn. Jimmy has joined them, sitting back in a garden chair, watching them as they run through the water. It's a sweet scene of apparently idyllic family life.

'The options are limited, but there are choices that you need to make,' the social worker continues. 'My sense is that in these circumstances a school move may well be a prudent choice.' His voice rolls onwards, as if this process of the choice, and the decisions I make around it, are things over which I have control. But control feels like something I gave up quite a long time ago. Usually, I feel as if the children have control, and I am simply running around after them, carrying a bucketful of water that's punctured with holes.

While he speaks, I put the phone on to hands-free so that I can press the flat of my palm into my shoulder. My nipples are still sore, and until they are completely healed they will send stabs of pain through my collarbone and up my neck. On the lawn below, Jimmy is now running through the sprinkler, holding hands with Dash to make him laugh more. It is wild, I think, for Dash to see someone as big and tall and *grown up* as Jimmy playing with him. He can't understand, of course, how young an adolescent is, how Jimmy is just as impulsive and headstrong as he is.

Jimmy is a marvellous surprise for Dash. He does things that are even more anarchic than the chaos of a toddler. Nothing makes Dash happier than seeing Jimmy climb out of a bedroom window on to the flat veranda roof of our house, or on up over the small gables to sit on the roof. Jimmy is strong and agile, and he knows that the risk isn't great, but to Dash it's the most daring thing in the world, and he loves it.

I watch them as if from a distance, just as the man on the end of the phone sounds very far from me too. Perhaps the man senses my distance, because he clears his throat, signalling that he needs an answer.

'Do you think he really has to move schools?' I ask. 'I mean, I know that smoking, and smoking weed, in school – it's wrong, of course, and that he needs to understand the consequences of this, but isn't something like this very common, very normal, for an adolescent boy?' As I speak, I realize that I don't really know whether it's even legal to be caught in possession of weed.

'We're talking about a zero-tolerance issue, Miss Stroud,' he replies, as if that explains everything.

I try to imagine zero tolerance at home and how it would work amidst the groundswell of family life. Being a parent involves suppleness in the way you think and behave. Every day, every passing year, requires so many compromises and changes. Nothing is set in stone, as far as I see, apart from love, which is carved in rock inside me.

'Of course you can appeal this decision, but should you do so, there's no guarantee he would keep his place. And once a new place is found, he could be sent anywhere in the county. If you decide not to appeal, the school can organize what is called a "managed move".'

Sitting on the edge of the bed, with the sounds of the kids coming from all ends of the house, I try to imagine Jimmy at a school at the other end of the county. Getting them all to school involves several different buses, and a lot of driving. It would be disastrous for Jimmy to have to be ferried miles away, too. It might break me. Until now, according to the school, Jimmy has been a good student. He has worked quite hard, got quite good grades and shown enough enthusiasm in most of his subjects to please his teachers, at least.

'Miss Stroud, we recognize this is Jimmy's first real misdemeanour in school. With a managed move, he'd start the autumn term at a new school and be given the chance to start again. None of the other students and most of the teachers even need to know why he has moved. A fresh start may be a great thing for Jimmy and I would strongly recommend it in these, er, difficult circumstances.'

The fall in the man's voice signals that the conversation is over. We agree to speak again in a few days, and I hang up. Lester turns his head towards me, and I reach down to him, cradling him against my shoulder. I will do anything to protect this tiny being, but that need to protect is just as strong for Jimmy, even if harder to manifest.

Of course, I have to disapprove. But I am not surprised, or shocked. Being a teenager – and being an adult – is messy and difficult; we make mistakes. There is no life without experimentation and certainly no life without mistakes. But in order to be a good mother, I have to pretend that I mind a whole lot more than I really do.

Downstairs, there is a huge crash followed by a deep silence, and then a scuttling of children's voices. At least I can still hear them all. Whatever has broken can't really matter; it can't be that serious. I cannot come running every time there is a crash. I wrap Lester in his muslin square, pressing him gently into his cot, trying not to gasp as I slather lanolin on my nipples.

In the kitchen, a poster of Matisse's *Snail* that I'd had framed several weeks ago, but had not got round to hanging, had been propped against the wall. Now it's lying face down on the wooden floor. When I pick up the picture, all the glass is lying in a perfect square but smashed into hundreds of tiny terrifying shards.

Jimmy pauses to examine it as he wanders back into the kitchen, telling me quickly it was Dash, not him, who knocked it over. Dash stops for a moment, naked, in front of me, clutching Playmobil figures in one hand and some track and a wooden Thomas in the other. 'It didn't bang,' he says. He looks at the broken glass, then back at the wall where the now splintered frame had been propped. 'It didn't break.'

I find a dustpan and brush, kneeling down carefully to sweep up the glass before small bare feet return; outside, Dash and Evangeline's voices are swallowed by the space of the garden and fields around them. This was what I wanted and what I had dreamed, when Dash was a newborn baby, and I'd lost my mind living in the city in a 1960s town house that was too small for my new husband and now four children. The kitchen and sitting room were on the first floor and the garden was an unfenced strip of grass outside the front of the house extending to a road that taxi drivers used to like speeding down.

I was a single mother when I bought that house, and it had felt like the greatest achievement of my life. It almost felt bigger than becoming a mother: you fall pregnant, but no one falls into organizing a mortgage. It was an ugly house but I loved the big weeping willow outside and the picture windows that flooded the sitting room with light. I'd conjured up this house entirely alone for Jimmy, Dolly and me, and it was home.

But then I met Pete, and we had Evangeline and Dash soon afterwards, and I wanted to reimagine motherhood in a new place. Suddenly, the house I'd loved felt like a prison. We had no real outside space and I craved the open expanses of my childhood for these new babies to grow up in. In a rush, we moved out of the city to a cottage near a railway track with the green fields of Oxfordshire close enough to touch from our bedroom window.

Jimmy and Dolly were growing up beyond the primary school gate into secondary school, but I was right back at the start of sleepless nights, sweet gummy smiles and first, faltering steps. Motherhood itself was tethering me again. In our new house, we had a garden where the children could run straight out from the kitchen, with fields all around us. I thought that in the country I'd be liberated. I hadn't realized that the feeling of entrapment couldn't be solved by fields, or space, but was a place I carried inside me. It was motherhood, more than anything, that brought me right up against it. Loving them is easy; it's pure joy. But being a mother, and what that demands of me, night and day until I feel like I have become an eclipse, is something else.

Sometimes it cracks me open and there are days when what pours out of me are tears.

Lester is a few weeks old when he starts doing a new sharper sort of cry I've not heard from any of my children before. It's rasping, even as I hold him on my shoulder, rocking him after a feed as I walk through the house, calling the children for supper, patting his little back, feeding him some more as they clamour around the table, Dolly dishing out sausages, rice and slices of cucumber that Dash and Evangeline immediately remove from their plates. My breasts and my milk do not comfort him now; his stomach is hard, his tiny face red with fury, clawing at the air as the animal sound of his cries fills the kitchen. He will only sleep under the crook of my arm, snuffling for a nipple as the morning hours arrive, so that my arm and back feel like a plank. I walk with him, rocking and stroking him all day, but my love and attention and body are no answer to his pain. Something round and perfect I was keeping in a secret place bursts, a silent pop inside me as despair alchemizes in the crucible of motherhood.

The optimism his birth brought with it subsides into the past. I was wrong to think that this time I could be the good mother I wanted to be to my children. It was a mirage. In fact, I am exactly the same woman I have always been. I am still irritable, detached, bored, impatient, frustrated. I had been pretending. I do not change.

I am not better, calmer, kinder, sweeter. And anyway, I do not know who I am any more; Lester cries so much and even at night there is no rest. I don't have time to figure it out.

When Jimmy was a baby, he also cried a lot, so when he was a few weeks old, I called my mother-in-law, who was a midwife. She is one of the calmest, kindest, most serene women I know, and I needed to ask her how I could make Jimmy stop crying. It was late, and I could hear a dryness in her voice that suggested she'd been asleep, which made me jealous. 'He will just cry. Just cuddle him and hold him. As long as he's not hungry, and hasn't got a dirty nappy, and he doesn't need burping, you know that you've done your job and everything you can possibly do to make him comfortable.'

'But why does he keep on and on crying even when I've done those things?' I asked, crying myself now, hoping she might tell me about a secret code to being a mother that I just needed to figure out to make everything right again.

'He's a baby. It's his way of existing. It's his way of being. Sometimes I think babies cry just to feel themselves. To feel the outside edges of themselves.'

Sixteen years later I want to call her again, even though I have been divorced from her son for many years. And while I am trying to work out why Lester is crying, that phrase, 'to feel the outside edge', resonates down the years. Perhaps that's why I cry, too: not because being a mother makes me feel sad, as I often cry when I'm happy, but instead to feel the outside edges of myself.

Lester cries and cries, almost incessantly, small legs and arms pedalling around like a lunatic. Reflux, says the doctor, and tells me that nothing will really help apart from time. As his digestive system matures, his pain will subside. The only way I can soothe him is to put my breast into the cavity of his dark crimson mouth and sit quietly with him, alone, ideally in a dark room without distraction, light or sound. Dash and Evangeline don't like my exclusion, hunting me out from my darkened rooms to crawl all over him like insects. Evangeline wants to hold him on her tiny lap where he scratches at the air. Dash wants to press his mouth very, very hard against Lester's. But Dash is solid and round, his godfather calls him Young Hercules, and I'm worried he'll break Lester, like he did the picture in the kitchen.

Often it feels as if no part of my body is mine any more. I want to enjoy every moment of this, but how can I when I am thick with exhaustion, my body wrung out, so that I have to call Dolly to protect me? She scoops them up with promises of fun and games outside, in the sun.

In between crying, Lester is sick. Eight or nine times a day, he pukes a tiny bellyful of breastfeed at me. I am perpetually covered in white vomit. I keep changing my T-shirt until the dirty washing banks up too fast and then I give up trying to keep clean since no one apart from Pete or the kids will ever see me now.

I love Lester with every cell in my body, but this is also really difficult. Sometimes I feel as though I'm shut in a wire trap. I know, I know: I've willingly shut myself in here, but this love has me encased, imprisoned, nonetheless. Walking Lester around the kitchen again, after

Pete has left for work, it's as if I can, in tiny flashes, see myself inside this cage, my body contorted as I struggle, the outside world visible through all the holes, but distant, vanishing. I do not want to use the words post-natal depression because I have felt the deep, dark, separate sadness of that, but I recognize the sense of uncertainty I'm feeling as something other than just exhaustion.

'You won't have it this time,' my friend Virgil says. 'You won't have post-natal depression again.' Virgil has long red hair with a blunt fringe and wears the kind of shirts with little neckties that country-music stars from Nashville wear. I like being near her. She makes me feel as if the 1970s of my early childhood are close enough to touch, because although in other ways she seems as if she is my age, she was actually a mother herself when I was born. When I'm with her, the sepia colours of old photographs seem to surround us.

I sit in Virgil's sitting room holding a hot little bundle of baby in my arms. She makes a cup of tea in a willow-pattern cup and puts some Rich Tea biscuits on a plate. Her voice is thick and soft: it reassures, like wine falling into a big green glass.

'No, it won't happen again,' she repeats, stirring her tea. 'You know what it feels like. You'll recognize it. This time, you'll be able to recognize it before it gets a grip and be able to see it off.'

I think of the red and white bull that stands by the cows, throbbing with masculinity, in the field by the house where I walk our dog, Pablo. Turning around to face that bull, to scare it away, would take courage.

Chasing off post-natal depression, and stopping my mind sloping back into that special groove of exhaustion and despair and distance that being with a new baby can bring, and which my mind has known so well, is hard work. It does take courage. And the ghoul of post-natal depression is only too ready to revisit me, if I don't resist. Keeping it at bay requires me to concentrate. When I feel tears rising in my eyes too quickly, or a blank sense of separation sliding between me and the rest of the world, I know the ghoul is close and needs resisting.

I have had it, twice before, after Evangeline and Dash were born. I had read that it is often caused by a traumatic birth experience, and because I'd had agonizing but very positive experiences, I might have thought I was safe. I was bonded tight to both babies, too, but still it came for me. My mother was still alive but very ill when Evangeline was born; she died when I was pregnant with Dash. Looking back it seems inevitable that I should have walked into a storm at this time, because mothering a baby when you have lost, or are losing, your own mother, is hard.

But I think the depression I experienced also came from the way I was straining to be a perfect mother to them. I wanted to be always calm, loving, benign and generous, and so when I also started feeling angry, frustrated, despairing or bored, I tried to deny it to myself until I felt as if I was drowning.

I thought that a mother should not feel despair. On an advert for yogurt drinks, I see a pretty, happy mother wiping a smudge of strawberry cream from her daughter's mouth and then smiling in a benign way. She doesn't frown or sigh. She isn't trying to do many other things at the same time and she doesn't get yogurt on her clothes, either. Dash and Evangeline watch a programme called *Topsy and Tim*, about a set of perfect twin children with kind-looking parents. The mother never, ever cries. She never shouts at Topsy and Tim at bedtime or ignores them to lie on her own bed weeping when they throw toys at her. She never behaves as if another slow afternoon alone with her children, when there might be so many other thoughts she could be having and lives she could be inhabiting, will actually kill her. She smiles in a distant but connected way, and yet she never smothers her children with kisses, or sniffs the back of their necks, or buries her face in their tummies, either. She never looks as if she wants to devour them. And while her hair always looks tidy and she manages to be in good shape without ever dieting, she doesn't look like she's ever had sex. She never stands in the kitchen silently eating one biscuit after another until three-quarters of a packet have gone while her children are watching YouTube next door and the sun shines outside.

I study her sometimes, when I'm feeding Lester, Dash and Evangeline curled up next to me in the afternoon heat. She's a mother before she is anyone, someone who is ceaselessly giving, constantly kind, enduringly patient and perennially benign. She is pastel-hued and pin neat, communicating gently, firmly, with her children. No means no and her children obey. She has authority but contains her extreme emotions, maybe because those are powerful and dangerous as a storm. There's no pain and rage in Topsy and Tim's mum.

The truth is that this calm, organized, sweet version of motherhood is not much like anything I have ever experienced. In fact, increasingly I think that the portrayal of motherhood in *Topsy and Tim* is a dangerously irresponsible piece of propaganda; it makes motherhood look like something quite different to how it feels in real life, and is almost as bad as a video to recruit Isis brides that suggests life in the caliphate is going to be about making date cookies in the sun while waiting for your warrior husband to arrive home. You give up your life and all your freedom, and when you get there, it's really terrible clothes, bleeding heads on sticks and bombs going off everywhere.

'For fuck's sake, Mum. Are you there?' Jimmy is standing in front of me, waving. 'Are you even listening?' I am sitting on the sofa in the kitchen, with Lester tucked into me like he's part of my body, and I feel distant from absolutely everything apart from him, until Jimmy's voice pulls at me. I look up quickly, trying to adjust my face to hide the fact that the answer to that question is no, I'm absolutely not listening.

I blink hard, as though that will make me connect, but all I can focus on is how tall Jimmy is, as if he's grown too big for the family.

'OK, I was wondering if you would let me go and see Matt tonight?'

Jimmy was supposed to be grounded, but it's so hot, this seems impractical. I can't ground him in midsummer. I cannot shut him in for ever.

'OK.' I nod. 'For a couple of hours, yes, yes, you can,' I reply slowly, shifting Lester under my arm. Jimmy brightens, as if he had been bracing himself for quite a different answer and this is a lovely surprise.

'Really? Wow. Great, thanks,' he replies. He clearly senses that he's got me because he goes on: 'What about a lift? Can you give me a lift there?' I nod again because I have no resistance. I am exhausted, not by the newborn baby, but by this role I've had to unwillingly adopt of being the constant, casual policewoman in the house. I do not want to guard or punish, and I do not want to enforce laws. Pete is away so much that when he comes home, he doesn't want to police. And Jimmy is mine. He's my son. It's my job, although I didn't think the intensity of my role as a mother would go on so long. I didn't think I'd still be having to monitor my teenage son as I do my two-year-old. Does this ever end?

'Thanks, Mum. I really appreciate that,' he says; then he stands in front of me for a bit before sitting down on the sofa, suddenly, beside me. We are silent together. He takes Lester's tiny hand in his own. Lester has pointed fingers and his skin overlaps and falls from his hands, too big for the bones inside it. Because he's so small, he needs to grow into his skin. 'Look, Mum,' says Jimmy softly, stroking the top of his brother's tiny hand. 'Skin gloves.'

'How's the new baby?' a mother standing at the bottom of the slide in the park asks me, nodding at Lester on my shoulder. At the swings, Dolly pushes Dash and Evangeline as they squeak and squirm in the metal seats, pleading with her to push them higher, faster, just one more time. Lester is a magnet: he draws people – at least the women – towards him with an invisible power.

'He's fine, he's great,' I say, smiling at her quickly because what she is really asking is if he sleeps. 'He's so sweet. He's had some reflux, so he's cried a lot, but that's not his fault. He's good.' I don't say anything about the yearning I have for him. I don't tell her about the feeling I sometimes get when I'm holding him, which is like I'm missing him, even when he's in my arms, even as I'm staring straight into his eyes. People don't want to hear that. They don't want to hear how terrifying love for your children can be.

The intensity of the way I feel petrifies me. Sometimes I think it comes from the wild violence and energy of labour. My mother love is not soft or gentle; it isn't pastel-coloured or decorated with bunnies and chicks, like the mother love you see in adverts for nappies or buggies. It's a wild love; it thrashes and roars. It's a massive, jagged emotion, coursing through my blood and covering my skin and seeping into my bone marrow. It's deep love but there's fear there, too. Becoming a mother has unleashed this feeling of intense new love, but it's also unleashed the possibility of a loss so great, I don't know how my body could contain it. My love for Lester, and for all of my children, hurts me, like a bruise under a nail, protected on the surface by the hardness of life but actually bleeding underneath.

Perhaps it's the softness of a newborn baby that brings this kind of love so sharply into focus. There were times, when the other children were very small, when I would take them to baby groups, looking for other women I could talk to about the new feelings of dark love which occasionally took hold of me. Sometimes I'd see a woman shaking a striped duck with a bell inside it in front of a baby who lay on its back, smiling, and I'd think that I'd found my girl. She would look different to the other women, who mostly seemed to be deliberately distracting themselves from the pain of motherhood by a persistent chat about maternity pay, or cluster feeding, or the merits of baby-led weaning over pureed food. I'd convince myself that she would be open to it, psyching myself up to go and sit beside her on another coloured mat, as though we were on rafts lost at sea, to try and entice her into chatting with a benign enquiry about how old her baby was. Sometimes I'd even find I could keep this conversation up long enough to create a sense that I really wanted to talk about baby-weaning and bed-sharing, or sleep schedules, or whether that new type of buggy was worth it. But I'd always seem to get it wrong, unable to resist a compulsion to ask the woman if she recognized this pain I was carrying at having given birth to a love so huge and terrifying it often seemed to overwhelm me. Or I'd completely blow it, just as I felt I might be making a new friend, by asking the mother if she had ever experienced the kind of invasive thoughts in which she might smother her new baby, stab her with a bread knife or throw her off a bridge. I stopped going to baby groups because I could never find the person I needed to talk to about these things. Voicing them amongst other mothers seemed to confuse everyone, and I learned that at baby groups it's safer to just go on singing pat-a-cake-pat-a-cake as if the feeling didn't exist.

'It's almost like a divine experience,' says Alex, her blonde hair a glowing halo around her head. Her daughter was born five days after Lester, by elective Caesarean, and at three weeks Alex thinks she is already starting to smile. Alex's mother stayed with her for the first two weeks, and her baby feeds easily. As she tells me about her labour, Alex's face is open, almost guileless, as if by talking about it she's returning to a place inside her that's truer than anything she's ever experienced. Her pale skin stretched tight across her forehead looks very thin, she's living with everything on the outside, and her lips are a little redder, her eyes brighter than normal, as if everything about her is hyper-sensitive. Both of us want to return to the memories of our labour again and again, and in one another we've found willing time travellers. Alex stands up, patting her daughter on her shoulder as she walks her around the kitchen. She's returned to her pre-baby shape, long and lithe and stretchy. 'Yoga!' she laughs when I comment on it. 'In the early morning, after she's just fed and I can put her back in her cot, I throw out a few sun salutations to keep my head together. It reminds me to breathe, too.'

'They're almost easiest when they're this small, don't you think? So much more portable and easier than when they start crawling,' I say. 'Which part of this early stage will you miss the most?'

'Oh, all of it! I'll miss all of it. Don't you just want to sort of grab them and keep them tiny for a bit? I can't bear her growing out of her newborn baby clothes. I can't bear the thought of being apart from her or of her being bigger. I just want to hold on to this strange enchantment of her being newborn.' She settles on the floor, tucking her legs underneath her, pulling a strand of hair back behind her ear as she gently lays her daughter on to the rug. Her daughter grasps her mother's finger, staring at her as if a line of taut thread connects their irises. Alex strokes the side of her daughter's face with her little finger. Then she says, 'Sometimes I feel worried about that. The way I only really want to be with her. Like I could cut myself off from the rest of the world and just vanish. And that that wouldn't matter.' She pauses again, as if she's trying the idea out on me. Lester has finished feeding, suddenly pulling his head back, eyes pressed tight shut, releasing my nipple.

'I sometimes feel as if having a baby is like joining a cult,' I reply. 'It's an experience I have willingly surrendered my life, my body, my mind, everything to. I have given myself completely over to it.'

Alex nods and gives a little laugh. 'And do you think that's because you can't leave it? You can't leave this cult? It has you under its spell?'

'Yes, something like that,' I say. 'Nothing pulls you to such extremes in a single day, does it? The highs and the lows are so . . . intensely confusing. If my emotional life was a temperature chart it would be spiking and dropping all the time. Unless I'm just on my own, feeding Lester, I never feel constant. I almost always feel all over the place. Turbulent but also very quiet.'

Alex looks up at me, her face empty and open at the same time, and nods at me. 'It's a terrible kind of love, the extremity of it, don't you think?'

Later, when I am home, I walk out into the garden, alone for the first time in ages. Lester is sleeping in his Moses basket in the kitchen, and Dash and Evangeline are watching a cartoon on my computer in bed. Dolly is in her room on YouTube, and Pete is away in London. We'd spoken on the phone earlier, and the tenor of our conversations was calming as we navigated through a plan for Jimmy's school move.

I take my shoes off and walk across the grass, feeling the end of the summer heat in the earth beneath me. Remembering Alex's advice, I consciously breathe in and out, wriggling my toes in the grass, trying to feel still. Maybe I don't need to worry about all these intense feelings, and it's enough just to have got to this point, to have fed Lester and soothed him and kept him alive for the past few weeks. Maybe that's all I have needed to do. Maybe I can relax.

I am clearing up mugs, clothes and plastic toys left around the garden in the last of the evening light when a car pulls up at the gate.

It's a police car. A real-life policeman gets out of the car. I put everything down and I walk over to him, to direct him to whichever house he must be looking for.

'Sorry to disturb you, but I'm looking for Jimmy's mum. Have I come to the right place?'

4

Playing with Knives

Before I had children, or at least, when I was pregnant for the first time, before Jimmy was born, and later, into his early childhood, this is what I imagined:

My children will only play with wooden toys.
My children will start foreign-language lessons when they are four.
My children will not shout in cafes.
I will never shout at my children in cafes.
I will never hit my children.
My children won't eat sweets before they are five.
My children will eat fruit or vegetables every day.
My children will always say please and thank you.
My children will never ignore adults.
My children will learn at least one musical instrument each.
I will read to my children every night.

I will teach my children to read fluently before
 they start school.
I will teach my children all their times tables off
 by heart.
My children will never swear at me.
I'll never swear at my children.
I will always love my children.

I have failed at all of these, apart from one.

And when the policeman is asking for me, I realize that
I am failing at lots more, newer, different things, too.
My failings are growing to match the size of my children. Because when I held newborn baby Jimmy, I
never saw a policeman in our future. I saw chubby legs,
babygros, sippy cups and wooden toys, cardboard reading books, packed lunch boxes, bunk beds, school shoes,
a family-size tent, a school bag and a pencil case full of
scented pencils. I never saw this, or this completely new
feeling of being conflicted about what my role in all
this is. The policeman, whose uniform makes him look
a bit like one of the Playmobil toys Dash and Evangeline
leave on the kitchen floor for me to tread on barefoot,
stands in front of me and is talking to me. I can tell,
immediately, from his stance and a slight softness in his
face, that nothing really awful has happened. Jimmy
isn't hurt; no one is dead. But still: a policeman.

So I watch his mouth moving, but it's as if my brain
has frozen in a single moment of sound and motion,
like the shuttered slam of seats being flipped upwards in
a deserted auditorium. I raise my eyebrows and smile at
him with my lips pressed hard together, but none of

this feels right. Should I be smiling at him like this? Should I smile with my teeth or with my lips shut? At this moment, I do not know how to rearrange my face or how it is I am supposed to be as a mother. None of the baby books suggested this was what was coming rushing up on the horizon. And although the policeman arriving is a surprise, it's not a terrible shock, because what I am trying to accept as my children get older is that motherhood is a drama that I will act out every day. I don't suppose this will be the last policeman in my life.

Often in the course of a single morning, a single hour, motherhood will take me to a place where I feel: This is the end of my tether. *This* place, right now, in the mess and chaos, is when I snap. *This* place is all I can take. *This* is my limit.

'I'm at the end of my tether!' I'll scream at the children, slamming a pan into the sink in an attempt to scare them into obedience. Or I'll wail at my sister, 'I can't take any more. Please, please come over. I'm at the end of my tether.' Or I'll text Pete: *When are you home???? End of my fucking tether.*

Being a mother pushes me, unwillingly, into parts of my mind that I didn't know existed before I had children.

These tests are different from other tests I've lived through. The pressures of caring for my children, making them happy, feeding them, educating them, cherishing them, trying to fashion a childhood that's happy as well as successful, authentic, loving and also woven through with my own memories so that it means something significant and enduring, often feels like being in a locked room that's filling with water. And the tests of motherhood are like a solemn responsibility. Am I getting this right? Am I doing enough? Am I a good enough mother, or barely close? And is *good enough* good enough, anyway?

So, you see, as the policeman stands there talking, every certainty I thought I might have held dissolves. I've been mothering for nearly sixteen years and thought I'd seen it all, but *this* is something new. I thought I'd reached the end of my tether completely with it, but it turns out there's always more rope to throw out.

'A knife? He had a knife, in school, when he was still in school? As well as the weed? Oh dear, that's not good. I mean I know he has knives, at home, but not in *school*,' I say, running one hand across my brow and through my hair, gazing down at the gravel beneath my feet, desperately searching for an answer there, arranging and rearranging my thoughts and face, and then making eye contact again.

'So you knew?' the policeman asks, his voice sharpening.

'Yes, I know, yes, of course. I mean I know he has knives,' I tell him. 'I mean Jimmy, well, he's been collecting penknives since he was much younger. Little penknives with wooden handles or engraved blades, usually things I bought on trips abroad for him, and once his godfather gave him a knife, and my sister bought him one in Portugal. And another time I was given a really big knife for him, when I was working in Russia, ages ago.' My words tumble out, making what I hoped would sound like a rational explanation into a careless mess. I try and think of something to make this all sound more considered. 'I'm a journalist, you see, so I was writing about Russia and I was given the knives as presents for my children, as they weren't with me when I was there as I was right down in the south. Of course they were at home with grandparents, I hadn't just left them on their own. And I took the knives home with me as little presents from a faraway land. To educate them. And so on.' Even to myself, I sound completely ridiculous. I clear my throat, stand up a little straighter to look him in the face and shrug off my guilt. 'And so, yes, I mean I've been giving him knives, since he was small, too.'

He stands square in front of me, his palms parallel to one another, pointing towards me. 'Can I get this right for a moment. You have been giving him knives? Since he was small?' he repeats, and I nod vigorously because I think that will clearly make it OK: if he's been given a knife by me, his mother, there can't be anything wrong, can there?

'I think that you should know that a minor carrying a knife is a very serious offence,' he says slowly. He's a zero-tolerance sort of policeman.

'Yes, yes, it is. Oh yes, of course it is,' I reply, because it's all suddenly dawning on me, as the look he gives me suggests that now, while he's concerned about Jimmy, he's also concerned about me, too. I'm thinking about this while I speak – about Jimmy, and being his mother and how I should have done this and that differently, but I'm also distracted by how handsome this man is, in a neat, clean, cropped way. And for a split second I can't help wondering what his skin would smell like with sweat and come on it and how he would move and what his body would feel like, because he could easily have stepped out of any one of the crappy porn films I sometimes watch on my phone in the afternoon, when the children are out with Pavel and I'm supposed to be working but feeling unfocused and the only thing that makes me concentrate is to come. At that moment, the thoughts of myself as a grown-up, responsible mother are delightfully distant.

'Miss Stroud, your son was carrying a knife – a throwing knife – at school. Which is a very dangerous weapon, the possession of which we take very seriously . . .' He stops, as though he's expecting me to say something.

'Yes. I know it's serious. But he's not carrying a knife in that kind of way,' I say.

'What do you mean?' the policeman asked.

'I mean this was one of the reasons we moved to the country, so that Jimmy could have a knife to kill a rabbit, or learn how to set a snare. He sets snares all around the fields here and occasionally kills rabbits, although not that often . . .' My voice trails off again as I suddenly realize I'm now potentially shopping my son as a poacher, which could also be something this policeman has zero tolerance for.

'A knife is an offensive weapon and clearly when carried by anyone it's serious, but by a minor, particularly so,' the policeman repeats.

Suddenly, I figure out how to rescue the situation. Leaning up against the fence separating the house from the big field next door I spy the large wooden target board with a bullseye in the middle of it that Jimmy uses for target practice.

'Look, look at this,' I say, running across the lawn to pick up the target and holding it in front of him. 'This is what the throwing knife was for. I was encouraging him to do target practice because it gets boring here. It's really boring for teenagers. In the middle of the country. I mean it's boring for me, a grown-up, so I've tried to imagine what it's like for a teenage boy, for Jimmy. He had asked me for a throwing knife so I bought him a set and we made this target together.' I stop, looking keenly up at the policeman, and watch him running his eyes up and down the wooden board decorated with a roughly drawn black and red bullseye marked out in bristly paint strokes, and all around it hundreds of holes and hacks made by a determined-looking knife-thrower. Perhaps too determined. There are so many holes the scene looks practically criminal. I look up at the policeman again and wonder whether he thinks Jimmy is a psychopath – and perhaps whether I am, too.

The policeman looks perplexed. Then he says he understands it's a teenage thing to do, but that this has to be taken very seriously. He will have to come back to talk to Jimmy at some point about the seriousness of the infraction, '. . . even if he is just using the knife to scare rabbits,' he says finally, as he heads back to his shiny police car.

I sense I have won the policeman over and success-fully defended my son, but as soon as I hear the car head off, I feel my loyalties scattered all over the place like marbles running across a wooden floor. I must pick my moment to speak to Jimmy, too. I must try to create an impression – to Jimmy at least – that zero

tolerance is something I, too, a woman without a uniform and the law behind me, will have enough pure
human energy to enforce.

Some days later, I drive Jimmy to Swindon to get uniform for his move to the new school. He's only come
with me to Swindon reluctantly, since he knows that
the drive will put him where he least wants to be,
which is trapped inside a car with me. He's had enough
of telling-offs. The policeman did come back the next
day, talking to Jimmy in a low, serious voice in his room
about knives and responsibility. As he left, Jimmy looked
briefly chastened, then scowled at me again. Everything
is my fault.

Now, he pauses at the front door before we leave,
looking tense, and I feel as if I'm coaxing a wild animal
into captivity, but then he realizes Lester is also coming,
which means he can sit in the back of the car, out of
earshot and beyond conversation. But when I clip the
baby seat into the seat behind mine and Jimmy understands the front passenger seat will be free, his face turns
downward and stormy.

The trust between us has plummeted. I can tell from
the way his throat tenses when he's around me that
Jimmy is wary of me pouncing on him, to interrogate
him and mine his teenage brain for crimes, real and
imagined. He's always ready, on the defensive, and when
I mention the knife, he's indignant. 'You know I'd never
use a knife on someone else, Mum,' he says.

By my silence I agree. I know it with an absolute
certainty because I once carried him as a baby in my
body. I even understand his indignation at this moment,

because the idea that he'd use a knife to hurt someone is madness. But this is not a straightforward situation either, since Jimmy flatly denies there is anything wrong with taking the knife into school. He was just giving it to a friend. 'Why do you have to get so mental about it, Mum? For fuck's sake, you don't understand me and you don't understand anything! You don't actually even care.' And he thumps the dashboard with a fully grown man's force.

Jimmy was a sweet, sweet baby, the child I met first, the boy who made me a mother. I've always felt I saw myself in him: I knew what he was thinking, what he was feeling, what made him happy; I could soothe his nightmares. The bond between us has been tight all his life; I understood his DNA. But something is changing, like a metal sliding door slamming shut in my face. For the first time, I can't get in.

His life, I am realizing with a jolt, is happening beyond the home and out of reach. His *real* life – the one he wants to inhabit rather than the one I've forced him to inhabit – is something I am no longer part of. His real life is now spent in places where I am not.

My life is spent mainly anxious about where the younger children are. 'Can you see Dash out in the garden?' I'll ask Dolly when I'm pinned to the sofa, feeding Lester, or I'll shout hysterically for Evangeline as I drain carrots through a colander if I haven't seen her for a while and a sudden fear she's fallen out of the window or been carried away by a passing car grips me out of nowhere. The younger children circle me, on the edges of my vision. I can always place them.

But Jimmy? He can just go. I may scream at him from the kitchen to come downstairs until my voice croaks, but all he'll reward me with is the sound of the front door slamming. I can bang on his bedroom door only to realize his room is empty and I've no idea where he is. He can simply walk out and there's nothing I can do to pull him back.

In the car, though, I have him trapped. And so, I try – again – to talk about knives and why he had had one in school.

'I was giving it to Tom.'

'Tom?'

'Yeah, you know, Tom. Tom!'

'Sorry, Jimmy, but who is Tom?'

'Tom! You know. Who lives near Swindon. The one I bought the knife for.'

'But I've never heard of him before.'

'Mum, what the fuck? You've *met* him. He was here a few weeks ago. And you knew about the knife anyway. I asked you! I asked you if I could use your card to buy it as I wanted to give him one. He wanted a knife and I said I'd give it to him.'

'You asked me? If you could give him the knife and use my card to pay for it? When? I don't have any memory of this at all.'

'Sometime. A few weeks ago. I don't know, just before Lester was born,' he says a little evasively.

'And what did I say?'

'You said yes, as long as his parents knew about it.'

I am quiet for a moment and then switch the radio off.

'Did I? Really? Did I say that?'

'Yes. I mean you did seem quite tired at the time, and you were trying to put the kids to bed. They were screaming a lot. It was just a normal evening. I asked you when the kids were in the bath. I mean I didn't come into the bathroom. I asked you through the door. You forgot! Like you forget absolutely everything! And now you're accusing me of lying to you.'

Sometimes, when Dash and Evangeline are in the bath, the room is so full of watery echoes and screaming that it is actually possible to entirely lose your sense of self.

'But you must have known I couldn't hear you. Why did you ask me then?'

'Why not then?' Jimmy returns.

There is silence between us, and then I say: 'And did his parents know about it? Did they know you were giving it to him?' Silence, again, before Jimmy shouts at me that I don't understand, I don't listen, and what's the fucking point as all I'll do is accuse him of things he hasn't done.

Our fury hangs in the car between us as we edge agonizingly slowly past roadworks, bumper to bumper with the car in front as the heat turns the concrete to a mirage. Jimmy shouts so hard at me his voice cracks. I say things to him I later despise myself for, things my father said to me once, during the only real argument we ever had, when I was the same age Jimmy is now, about disappointment and failure.

'Selfish and thoughtless, with no sense of responsibility to anyone but yourself.' They are horrible words which echo back to me across time, and now fall out of my mouth. The rage I feel towards Jimmy for pushing me out of his life quivers like a kinetic force in the car, and he turns his face right away from me as I say things that take me to a place I never wanted to be as a mother.

I rub my face, trying to push away the ill feeling, when a memory comes to me of Jimmy three years ago, a much younger boy, just twelve or thirteen, asking me to play ping pong with him or watch him on his skateboard. I had been so tired. I'd said no. Tomorrow, let's do it tomorrow, I'd said and he'd nodded. As I watched him walk out into the garden alone I told myself he didn't mind, not really, even though it happened all the time when he was a young teenager. I had a new baby, then another, and then another, throughout Jimmy's teenage life, and I was always sleepless. He had wanted my attention and my time and I'd turned him away, and now we are here, with this expanse between us in the car. Despair claws inside me, making me want to rip at my skin, because is it so hot, and the traffic won't move, and how did my little boy and I, my boy I was conjoined to, get to this awful point, so far apart from one another? I stretch my hands out on the steering wheel and I think I might start sobbing. Then the car inches forward once more, and a bank of colour is revealed on the roadside in front of us.

The colour comes from wildflowers, studding the exhausted grey, parched grass with a spattering of deep yolk yellow and a familiar blush of campion petals. Campion is one of the very few plant names I know, because it grew in the verges and hedges around our home when I was a child. Its bright pink petals are not easy to forget. They're the flower shape Evangeline will draw, hand smudging over the paper, before she can even write her name properly. There is no complex stamen, just tear-shaped petals in a colour I'd painted on a bedroom wall.

Jimmy also looks at the roadside flower festival. The colours are so vivid, they're almost impossible to ignore. 'Look,' he says, indicating the bank with his head. For the briefest of moments we catch one another's eye. In the back of the car, Lester stirs, and makes a quiet, pained noise that probably means he's hungry. Jimmy looks away from me again, and the traffic edges forward.

If the baby and teenager pull me to opposite ends of my tether, sending me swirling into a blur of anxiety about what I've done wrong in the past, and how I might be getting it wrong for the future, Dash lives his plump, noisy life in the absolute present, surround-sound volume turned up to max. He is like a cartoon character, a young Fred Flintstone or Desperate Dan. His feet are almost square and his temper and his heart are like his body: huge and round and irrepressible. He will push Lester away from my breast to clamber on to my lap clasping a book on deep-sea creatures, his square fat hands spread out over the page of black and white killer whales, panting with anticipation about what he will find there. He scratches at the pages, trying to touch the fish within them, and then he is furious, slapping the pages in rage, because there are no pictures of these whales actually killing someone. 'Stupid!' he'll shriek.

When I shrink down to his level to spread train tracks all over the kitchen floor, he'll ask me to pile up the carriages to make a huge crash. At night, he wants me to kiss each of his fingers, and touch the end of his nose so that he can see it. He sticks his red lips out for me to kiss them, and makes himself giggle heartily when he realizes he can see those, too, if he sticks them out far enough. When I think he's ready to sleep, and might just relax into the bed, a look of thunder passes across his face, his body under the duvet tensing, his legs and toes hitting the bed.

'Where are my eyes? I can't see my shiny blue eyes,' he wails, forcing himself out of the bed and flinging himself on the floor.

Everything about Dash is big and round. His body is brown and soft, big eyes set in a huge skull, and a round soft stomach. 'I want something chocolatey,' he'll say at breakfast, and he likes to eat biscuits in a stack of four. If I deny him sweets from the shop when we go to the park he'll cry and cry. 'I can't help it, I just love them so much.'

He is irresistible and impossible. Like Mum in the Oxford Reading Tree Biff and Chip books, with her crap hair and stripy jumpers, and her constant vague grimace, Dash often makes me wail, 'Oh no!' Yet I forgive him almost everything, and when I kiss him good-night, I want to nuzzle him, exhaling kisses into his neck, trying to imprint on my heart and mind this little boy that Dash is right now. I am an animal, licking my young as a manifestation of my love for them. My teenage child is the reminder that my relationship with this little boy, who cuddles me so tight I can barely breathe, is only here for a short time; a reminder that love in this form will disappear. In ten years' time, I will have lost this little-boy version of Dash, and someone else will be here in his place, someone who looks and seems a bit like him, but who in many ways is unrecognizably different. Once Jimmy was a little boy like this, who carried toy cars in his hot hands, and kept Digestive biscuits under his pillow, and liked to scribble because he said it made him feel fast. Sometimes the days of being a mother to toddlers is almost horrifically boring, but their passing also terrifies me. I don't know how to hold on to the days and the magic of innocence and happiness they contain. These days pass so slowly, but are over too fast.

I once read that a fourth child is the easiest, since by the time they are born there's not enough attention to go around. They are simply forced by circumstance to go with the groove of family life, to fit in. But Dash is the fourth child, and it's as if being placed so far along the pecking order of my attention has created in him an urgent need to be seen and heard and acknowledged. He pushes the others aside as if swiping objects off a table. Sometimes he screams so much, and with such force and passion, I have to restrain him. When he lashes out, screaming and kicking at the injustice of having to leave his train tracks to get into the bath, or the wrong I am doing him by making him get out of the bath to hear a story before bed, I will hold him in order to try and quieten him. Dash's tears squirt from his eyes and then bounce down his plump cheeks like a child's in a picture book.

I hold him because I feel guilty, too, because Dash didn't always scream like this. He was the smallest and quietest of all my newborn babies, lolling in my arms and difficult to wake for a feed. I always thought that babies come out fully formed, with their whole personality in place, but now when I look closely at photographs of the newborn Dash, so small and fragile, I wonder if something changed in him, that day when he was two weeks old, when I took him to the health visitor, anxious about whether it was normal that he was so small and thin and sleepy.

'I'm not saying it's meningitis,' the health visitor said, her face tightening as she examined Dash's sleeping body, laid flat on my lap, arms flung outwards, skin a little too hot. 'But . . . he needs to go to A & E immediately.' The walls of the windowless room seemed to close tighter around me and I was shaking when I called Pete outside. 'Meningitis . . . hospital . . . emergency': the words tumbled one over the other into a hideous pile, a single, silent 'NO' rising inside me.

At A & E two doctors unfurled him on a bed, examining his little body, before summoning the neurology department. Dash screamed as I held down his arm and a needle pierced his baby skin. Pete stroked the soft hair on his tiny head, whispering reassurances, but his eyes dark and scared, flicking to me quickly when we were told there was no question of Dash going home, but that I could stay in hospital with him, so he could be monitored.

Pete left to be with the other children, and that evening, I sat alone with Dash in the ward, pale blue evening light filtering through the patterned curtains hanging between the beds. There was no one else in the ward and it was almost as though we'd been forgotten, until a student nurse in a pale-blue tunic over black trousers came to sit with me while I fed Dash again. She said I should try expressing milk, 'so you can see exactly what you're feeding him. He might be a very hungry boy when he wakes up,' she said. She was big, a soft, calming presence beside me, stilling some of the anxiety I felt about how urgently the neurologists had examined Dash.

In the morning, more doctors prodded Dash, sticking needles in his tiny veins, taking more blood for tests. They talked about viral infections, but none of the tests brought back any clear results. I wanted to take him home, but on the third night a new doctor arrived to tell me Dash needed a lumbar puncture.

'We need to assess if he has a disease of the central nervous system,' he'd explained as the floor seemed to plummet away. 'Most usually, this can be in the spine or brain.' A few days before I'd been cloaked in the strange, deep joy of being a mother to a new baby but this was ripped away, replaced by a cold dagger of fear. Brain damage. I wanted to grab Dash and run, far away from the hauntingly empty ward and the plastic squeak of rubber shoes on the floor as the doctors paced around. I wanted to shake the doctors until they told me what any of this really meant: there were so many questions and no answers at all.

'It's going to be upsetting,' a nurse told me, explaining that he would have a needle inserted into his spine. 'He'll be fine without you and I can bring him straight back.' But I refused to give him up, and had to hold his tiny body down while the needle went in; he screamed like never before.

It still wasn't enough and they wanted more of Dash's blood. A tense female doctor told me that because his veins were exhausted, she'd need to take blood from a vein on Dash's skull. She didn't make eye contact with me, staring at a far point on the wall of the tiny, airless room where he was being examined again. He was alert, his head pushed right back as he stared around the room. Night and day had melded together like dirty plasticine in the artificial light of the hospital ward; the doctor looked as tired as I felt, and I had a strong instinct that no one should stick a needle into Dash's head.

'No, you won't do that,' I said, suddenly furious and certain I needed to protect him. I told her I'd feed him all night and that if there were more tests, they could be done in the morning.

The next morning, the tests finally came back completely clear. There was no viral infection, no meningitis. Dash and I went home, but something awoke in him during those days in hospital. Now, I wonder if I should have been more assertive. I was sure that Dash didn't have meningitis. I didn't have a test to prove it, but I just knew. Should I have stood in the way of those doctors and their needles? Is this why he screams now? I love Dash with the ferocity he demands, but when I'm holding him as he screams at me, the thought that I should have done something different, to protect him when he was a baby, slides silently behind my eyes and lodges there, like a piece of grit against my eyeball that I can't rub away.

The long days of late August cast a sweaty spell over family life. The kitchen doors to the garden are always open, and the garden outside is littered with the quietly deflating paddling pool, wet towels the colour of ice creams, and discarded badminton racquets. The house is constantly noisy, as if we're living inside a soft-play centre, or a busy cafe, since Jimmy cooks himself fried breakfast at least twice a day.

A neighbour once said living beside us was like being next door to Sicilians: there was always someone leaning out of the window shouting at another outside, a sense of babies in buggies and wet washing both waiting for attention, a house where there was often the sound of fighting or a plate smashing but raucous laughter, too. In the summer holidays Dash screams with the pure delight of waking up again as Dash, to spend his days making a runway between the paddling pool and the freezer, where he rummages around for ice lollies among the spilt bags of frozen peas and prawns. He and Evangeline wriggle from my grasp as I try to slather sun cream on to their arms and shoulders, to drag cushions and blankets out across the lawn for ever more elaborate dens and camps and plans. Evangeline is a natural leader, marshalling Dash with a notepad and scribble of writing about the cafe and pet shop she's planning to open outside. Pavel entertains the children by setting up a water slide using washing-up liquid on plastic bin bags, and Dolly wanders through the kitchen, trying on new bikinis and showing me different ways to plait her hair. She takes Lester, too, walking around with him since it's too hot for him to be outside that much; much of the time I spend with him is in shaded rooms, the blinds drawn down, the sound of the children outside.

Jimmy and I step around each other: avoidance is easier than confrontation. Keeping Jimmy caged at home is next to impossible, and nor do I have the heart for it. He goes out a bit, to see friends, but only during the day for a few hours. His sixteenth birthday passes with a family picnic by the river. He looks glum, and I am in agony. I try to make it fun, with a barbecue and a handful of his cousins, but I know exactly where he really wants to be, and it's not here, with me controlling him. My attempts to explain to him that this is what must happen in this process of growing up are clumsy.

'I'm the same as you. The things I have wanted are the same as the things you want now,' I've said, but he just stares at me blankly.

Nevertheless, some of the drama and recrimination of the month since the policeman came round has passed. Occasionally, we even pause to talk in the kitchen after the kids are in bed, when he wants some slight reassurance from me about what it might be like starting a new school in the middle of his GCSEs. In those moments a kind of closeness returns, just for a few minutes, before we drift away from each other again.

I am anyway almost completely disabled by Lester. He remains plastered to me; holding him, stroking him – loving him – seems to soothe the pain of the reflux that makes him cry so much. Most of that time is a blur of movement and feeding and burping and sleeping and changing and movement and feeding again. I try to just give myself to it. These days will pass, the voice in my head tells me, when an urge to get into the car and just drive away takes me. When these days are gone, I will miss them, I have to remind myself, when I feel completely lost to my children.

When the days were newly hot in early summer I thought I'd not tire of seeing Dash naked at breakfast again, but by early September I'm ready for the rituals of the new term. I love the smell of Evangeline's sun-streaked locks but by day thirty-five of the summer holidays I secretly welcome the trip to the hairdresser to cut the tangles out of her hair, to make her ready for term time and an order that will return to the house. I take her to WHSmith in Oxford, as a treat, to buy new pencils, a case decorated with ponies and a notebook covered in kittens. It's a small ritual, which returns me to my own childhood in a rush so sharp I have to force tears down when Evangeline slips her hand into mine as we walk back to the car, telling me that she's just a tiny bit afraid of moving to a new school. I kneel down at her level, shoppers passing around us, smoothing her tamed hair back from her perfect face. I tell her it will be a whole new world of exciting friends and kind teachers, and she marshals a fresh expression that combines determination and trepidation mixed together. A brand-new part of Evangeline's life is opening up. In moving to school, she is moving away from Dash, who will do half-days of pre-school. She sets up a desk in the room she shares with Dash so she can use her new notepad to practise her name in tall, spidery writing, turning over a clean page to start again as soon as she gets to the end of the word.

Dash fills every room he enters with his noise and demands, but Evangeline walks into a space and wants to work out how she can make it better. Her mind is fast and inventive, creating new order amongst the mess created by her younger brother. Sometimes I think she has much more power over Dash than I do, as he runs after her, playing her games.

'You can be the child and I'll be the mum and we're going on a shopping trip but first we have to drive to the seaside to buy ice creams for everyone,' I hear her telling Dash as they move through the house, gathering up dolls, blankets and endless bags they sling around themselves in an imitation of urgency.

'Ice creams? For who?' he asks brightly as Evangeline pauses, motioning to the dolls they are both holding.

'For my girls! Ice creams for all my babies, my girls,' she says, as if it's so obvious. I worry that dressing her in school uniform will entrap some of her restless creative energy, but more than anything I want her to enjoy school. I want her to be happy there.

The start of term is always a shock. Suddenly Jimmy and Dolly must be on the school bus which stops near our gate by 7.45 a.m., but then the real exertion of will begins. My voice and blood pressure rise exponentially from 8 until 8.40, during which time the younger children will run around me in circles as I yank them into their clothes, coerce them into opening their mouths just for a moment so that a toothbrush might touch at least some of their teeth, persuade them to let me run a brush over the top of their tangles, remind them that cereal is for eating rather than spilling all over one another, and then shout at them to hurry up again and again and again so that we can at least have a vague chance of leaving the house on time, carrying book bags which almost certainly won't contain the worksheets they were supposed to do the previous night. Worksheets along with permission slips and the endless stream of missives which come from the school – Bring in a jar of sweets for the raffle! Don't forget the signed permission slip for the school photo! ALL children MUST come to school with a named water bottle, sun cream and sun hat EVERY day! Come to astronaut training club to see what the children have been up to all week! – can almost all be guaranteed to self-combust as soon as they get into the kitchen, itself a Bermuda Triangle of missing library books, school shoes, reading journals and parking fines. I'm genuinely excited when Aldi starts selling school shoes and I never have to go to Clarks again, because a lost shoe when it's only three weeks old is still lost, whether it cost £5.99 or £49.99.

Arriving at school on time is never down to anything other than luck, but in the classroom Evangeline's new teacher greets us on her first day, beaming.

'Hello, Evangeline. Your bag goes there and water bottle in the box. That's right, good girl, in the box,' she says, her face shining behind her large glasses, absolute heroine of the everyday. She smiles at me and another parent hovering on the classroom steps behind me. 'Here we go again,' she says, and I'm not sure if it's directed at the mothers or the children, but there's no time to answer before another parent deposits another child, its heart beating outside its school shirt, into her care.

A mother I recognize with a daughter in an older class is crouching before her son, who is hyperventilating, screaming, 'DADDDDDDDDY!' His face turns purple.

She's kneeling in front of him, repeating calming words to him as if talking a jumper down from a suspension bridge. She's wearing purple Lycra gym clothes, but the energy around her seems to have already left the playground. I know she doesn't want to be there: there's nothing like your own child clinging to you at the school gates to leave you feeling drenched in a toxic mixture of hottest guilt at your child's pain alchemized with purest irritation that they should be behaving as if you are sending them into the lions' den, rather than into the calm, creative and deeply kind arms of Mrs Roberts.

I was in my twenties when I first went to the school gate as a mother with Jimmy and Dolly. Back then, I always felt surrounded by married couples, putting my single-motherhood into stark relief. It was the mothers with partners who met for coffees, formed book groups and greeted one another in gym kit to go running together. I never felt as though I belonged: I just wanted to run away.

Now I'm past forty and Dash and Evangeline and later Lester are taking me back to the primary school gate. Secondary school is a different experience; children take themselves to school, so there are no play dates or fledgling relationships with new mums to navigate. Until that call summoning me to the headmistress's office, my dealings with Jimmy's school had mostly been at arm's length, confined to a call with the school receptionist confirming that the sports fleece that costs £58.99 online isn't an obligatory part of PE kit, an evening of speed-dating teachers through parents' evenings, and the occasional email from a form tutor about a piece of missed homework.

Primary school is much more intimate, an apparently benign gathering of parents and teachers we must all attend every morning in order to deposit our children in class at the right time, but which can feel like one of the loneliest places on earth; now I'm older I still feel on the outside, separate. I'm not good at the easy chit-chat the school gate demands; I can't do the plaits or high ponytails with matching scrunchies and clips like better-organized mothers, and we're always teetering on the edge of missing the school register.

At the school gate I watch other mothers and marvel at them. It makes me feel confused, as if my peers have found the right answer and I still don't really know the question. I look at them pushing clean buggies and I don't know how they manage that. All of the equipment around me that I use to transport or contain the babies – for example, the buggies and car seats, the high chair, the travel cot – have smears of mud or marks of food on them. I understand why the buggy is muddy, since I practically live in a field. But the travel cot? And at the school gate I'd like to be the mother who has had the forethought to bring a Tupperware box of cut-up chunks of raw vegetables and cheese to take to the park as a snack. Occasionally I find a twist of broken Digestive biscuits, like dry sand, in the bottom of the buggy. The children pounce on them anyway, mashing the crumbs into their faces. Sometimes I feel like a Glastonbury survivor, the red face of the baby tucked behind a fraying crochet blanket, one shoe fallen off, looking confused and hungry and at the end of a very long trip.

I constantly feel wrong-footed, muddled, disorganized around other mothers, but I don't want Evangeline to feel this. I try not to mind about the fact I know I won't be part of a WhatsApp group of other mums in class, but after I have admired the name tag on her peg, checked she has her full water bottle and kissed her on the cheek, inhaling something of her before school swallows her, I walk back out of school, quietly counting down the number of years I'll be at the primary school gate until Lester finishes. I tell myself that eleven years will go in a flash, and then I'll miss it.

After the school gate, the morning stretches out like a beach when the crowds have left: a relief, but lonely, too, and with a lot of litter that needs picking up.

I finish some toast left from Dolly's breakfast and, when Lester needs changing, Dash accompanies me upstairs, pausing carefully on every step as I walk behind him. Back in the kitchen, he empties his trains out from a giant basket with a huge clatter, making Lester cry. I feed him, change him again, kiss him on the back of his neck until he's sleepy enough to be pressed back into his cot. Back in the kitchen a second time, Dash appears at my side. 'Make track with me,' he says, insistent.

I look into his lovely face, wiping a smudge of brown chocolate from beside his mouth, but find his hands and cheeks are covered in a tacky, shiny film of something like sugary water or watery honey. Just looking at Dash makes me feel sticky, and there is a crunch of sugar under my feet. On the worktop beside the sink, there's a trail of honey, too. I locate further evidence: a Nutella pot lies on its side under the kitchen table with a knife protruding from it. Meanwhile flakes of Weetabix are strewn across the table like confetti, a cereal packet is discarded under a chair and plastic dolls lie face down across the floor, train track is mixed up with plastic farm animals and wooden blocks, and pens missing their lids scatter the play-table, as though some-one deliberately hurled them there.

Pete is at work and Pavel is at language school. I'm the only adult in the house. No one will actually notice, or care if they do notice, whether there's Weetabix all over the kitchen, and up the walls, too. Dash, in fact, probably prefers the random anarchy of this environ-ment to a well-ordered kitchen.

The fact that the demands of Dash and Lester will stuff every moment of this empty day with sticky, screaming need fills me with a dark reddish-blue despair, like the colour of a lobster before it's been cooked alive.

I make coffee, wiping away apathy on the sides in the kitchen, before Dash repeats his demand: 'Mum . . . Make track with me.' Resistance is futile: he won't move until I obey. I sit down next to him and he pushes the small carriages along, lost in deepest concentration to the demands of Thomas and Diesel. Our breathing is the only sound I can hear above the tick of the kitchen clock. Time settles around us, as invisible and quietly uncomfortable as lightly falling rain.

*

Until there were children, time was an endless resource I could bend to my will. Mostly, time was there to take me deeper and deeper into adult life. Of course there were traps, too: I have always thought of my life as broken into two: the time before I was sixteen, and the time after. I was sixteen when Mum dropped me at school, then went out riding on her horse. I was called out of a lesson, mid-morning, by the headmaster, who told me Mum had had an accident. My sister was there to take me to the hospital to see Mum; I thought it might be a broken leg and concussion, or maybe – which would be terrible – she had broken her back. I thought life would be disrupted but then it would resume as normal. But normal ended that day. Mum had fallen on her head, and was in a coma for several months. When she woke up, she couldn't talk or communicate in any way, and she was very disabled. She could never look after herself again. She lived at home with us for a bit, but then she went into rehabilitation centres and, later, nursing homes, where she lived for twenty-two years unaware of who I really was, until she died in 2013. Her accident totally rearranged all the windows in my life, boarding some up while replacing others with trapdoors, and flinging totally new ones open to reveal views I'd never seen before. All this left me with a hunger for a past that was gone, and a life, with Mum in it, that I'd never experience again. The future was there, too, looming as a longed-for moment when my real life – not the pretend one I was traipsing through – would actually start. This real life would kick into gear when the really important things I wanted started happening. These included holding a child of my own, writing a book, being in love with someone who loved me strongly back, having my own home, losing weight. The past and present were there. But if ever I thought about time, it was only to recognize that it was something moving me from one point to another.

Back then, time wasn't a puzzle. It didn't torture me with dizziness, constantly changing speed, and neither did it thrum behind my eyes, like a mild migraine, like it does now, tick, tick, ticking away, counting down, counting forward, as it has since Jimmy, Dolly, Evangeline, Dash and Lester stepped into my life.

People talk about having a baby to silence the ticking body clock, but in my experience having a baby just makes another clock tick more loudly. Jimmy switched on a timer which has been getting louder with each new baby. I am always counting, backwards and forwards. He's two weeks old, she's going to be three and a half, she's six and he's nine, she's going to be twelve! How can he be fifteen? Sixteen? How did that happen? I thought I had an endless source of it, but where has that time gone?

I do not want to cling to Pete, but his vanishing outline as he leaves for work at the start of the week, often not returning until the end of it, makes my heart plummet. I don't want to stand on the doorstep pleading with him not to leave me alone, but inside that's what I'm doing. I do not want to be ungrateful for what I have, but I also do not want him to go. Later, when he gets home, he'll ask me how the week was, and I'll really try and say: Oh, you know, fine, it was great, we did this, that and the other, and it was all really interesting.

He doesn't actually want me to communicate what being at home all day with a newborn and a pre-school child is really like; and neither do I fully know how to articulate the joy and claustrophobia of this, or the fact that while someone has been with me the entire time, touching me, prodding me, pulling at me, I have felt acutely lonely. I cannot describe how, while there's been a huge amount of noise, there's also been a deafening silence in my head. I cannot tell him that I felt time had not just stood still, but actually moved backwards, but that I'd also had too little of it to myself, that looking after the children had made me feel like an overfilled cup on a swaying table, slopping and spilling everywhere. He'd think I'd gone mad if I described how intense my longing was for this moment in my life to be over, while also feeling cauterized by a quiet sort of grief as I'd sorted through Lester's outgrown baby clothes.

How can I explain to him the tricks my mind plays on me by telling me that I don't like the toil that motherhood has forced on me, while quietly pondering whether a sixth child is out of the question? I don't know how to tell him that nothing happened all day, but that that sense of nothing was also completely overwhelming. Describing my disconnect from other women at the school gate, or women I see in the park pushing babies on a swing, makes me sound so unfriendly, and yet a chat is all I want. He won't understand how baby groups make me feel as if my heart has been scooped out and replaced with an excoriating sense of loneliness, or that the endless comparisons they can involve of whose baby is rolling over, reaching for a toy or sitting up unaided can seem a little pointless by the time you get to your third, let alone fifth, child.

I can't tell him how much the repetition that motherhood brings to every day can feel as though it may break me: some women claim there's a silence around the pain of labour, but there's a silence as loud around the squashed feeling of despair that can come with cooking supper which will get thrown into the bin untouched, night after night. I don't want to sound pathetic or, quite honestly, deranged, because just as strong as all these feelings is a sense that loving my children is the only thing that really matters in my life.

Instead I explain it like this: when Dash sits down and scribbles on the inside of a sticky cookbook, shouting, 'ZIGZAG, ZIGZAG,' I think he's describing what I've become. A day with the children when they are very small makes me feel like a zigzag.

A sliver of blonde hair and pale skin, Evangeline suddenly appears beside me in Jimmy's room. Moments before she'd been in the kitchen, small hands moving fast, creating a blended family from Sylvanians and Playmobil. I thought she was occupied. She has come up the stairs silently.

'Are you looking for fleas?' she asks, her face stern, her features still.

I pause, standing up straight suddenly from where I've been running my hands under the pillow and flicking his duvet back.

'Yes, exactly, fleas. That's what I'm looking for. Fleas,' I reply, relieved by the sweet innocence of her mind.

What I'm really looking for are Rizlas, small plastic packets, a grinder, tiny enamel boxes for keeping weed in jeans pockets, and lighters. The house has been so still and quiet, Jimmy's room was so beguilingly empty, that I'd paused at the top of the stairs outside the door and abandoned the pile of laundry I'd been hugging. I stepped into his room. A green smell of Lynx mixed with sweat and something foreign and sharp hit me as I stood by his desk. It might have been weed. Or hormones. It was something unidentifiable that only teenage boys smell of.

There were tubs of pencils, some notes, a photograph. I ran my hand over the desk, and then over his laptop, pausing there. I'd read Jimmy's emails in the past. Once, he'd used my phone to log into Facebook, and left his account open. Until he discovered his mistake a few hours later, I read all his messages. He spoke to his friends in a language I didn't understand, characterized by abbreviations and initials. If he had kept a diary, I would have read that too. If I knew how to use Snapchat properly, and I had the chance, I'd get on that too.

Do you blame me? I know, I know: I shouldn't spy on my child. I should respect his privacy, allow him boundaries, give him space, all that sort of thing. I know this is true, but when your teenage son stops talking to you, these messages beamed around the planet offer vital clues that can be used to piece together the strange new picture of the person your child has become. What you find might surprise or scare you; it might haunt or disgust you; it might even amuse you! The things I am looking for are also the clues I can use to make sure

Jimmy is safe, and that he is not doing himself any real harm. This is my life as a mother of a teenage boy.

And as the mother of a teenage boy intent on putting as much distance as he can between us, I'm charting a path as difficult and foreign as that of the new mother. There are sleepless nights, just as there were when Jimmy was a baby, and a strange new world to decode. Just as I do with Lester, I'm worrying about Jimmy's developmental charts, about how much food he's really eating and what its nutritional content is. Once again I'm searching, furtively, for slight changes in his skin colour, his smell, his ability to focus. He and Lester are bound to one another by a thin, invisible thread: oldest to youngest, the boy to the baby, each reaching out in his own way, as they go on their way to new worlds far away from me.

Beautiful Evangeline, meanwhile, walks around Jimmy's room beside me. She has my full, albeit guilty, undivided attention.

'I've seen some rabbits for sale. Me and Dolly looked on the internet. Can we get them?'

'Err. Yes. Maybe. Soon,' I answer, relieved that she hasn't seen I'm hunting for something quite different. 'I have the feeling a pet rabbit is the perfect thing to get, very soon, not right now, but soon.'

'Also, does Jimmy know he has fleas in his room?' asks Evangeline.

I smooth the duvet back, patting the pillows down, clattering together a handful of dirty mugs stained with tea from beside his bed.

'I don't think he knows he might have fleas in his room. Let's not tell him, shall we? Just so that it doesn't upset him. I mean, would you want to sleep in a bed with fleas?'

Evangeline looks at me sternly. I feel guilty. 'Shall we go and look at this rabbit? And see if we can find a cage second hand?'

Buying her a pet might be a way to appease the shame sweeping over me. I suddenly feel as though I'm lying to them all, pretending I know what I'm doing, pretending I'm the endlessly patient, endlessly engaged, endlessly kind mother from the children's books.

Dolly appears in front of me and tells me about her Spanish homework. I pretend to listen, but actually my brain is focused on something very different, very far away in Jimmy's future. Most of the time, in fact, I'm barely holding it together. The pace is relentless.

At the shop near our house, the lady who works in the post office asks me how old Lester is. When I'd taken him in there to buy sweets for the children when he was just a week old, she'd almost thrown herself across the counter to have a cuddle with him. I'd handed him to her as Dash and Evangeline grabbed my hand, dragging me down to eye level with the chocolate buttons and drumstick lollies. She'd inhaled him, pressing her face against the soft top of his skull. 'Oooh, it takes me back. I always wanted mine to stay like this when they were young, just at this age,' she'd said, and for a second I'd felt like she'd squeezed my heart. The time won't come around again – enjoy every moment, I'd thought to myself.

Now he's three months, I tell her.

'It's gone so fast,' she says. 'He'll be at school before you know it.'

She doesn't mean this unkindly, but what she says ends the newborn world I've been living in with Lester. The trance is over. He's not brand new any more. The zigzag muddle comes back. Folding his tiniest babygros and cardigans away to take to a charity shop is disturbing, as if something has been lost. Just as I want him to grow, I also want Lester as a newborn baby back. Time is tricking me again, and he's always moving away from me, the essence of who he is just outside my grasp, and I am left wondering whether this difficult yet intoxicating experience of mothering a newborn baby is something I'll ever feel again. I fear that in this trance I may have missed out on something serious and important about mothering that will never happen again.

5

Russian Beauties

Lester has started to leave bigger gaps between the times he is awake in the night. Sometimes I get to sleep for as long as four and a half hours in one stretch. That sleep is like strong medicine, bringing with it a clearer perspective on who I am. It helps me start to feel the outline of myself again. With pillows propped up around him, Lester can sit up and look around, head bobbing like it's on a string. In the kitchen I wedge him up on a blanket spread out on the floor and he scrapes his tiny hands against the rug, as if the wool itself were infinitely fascinating, before slowly toppling over, an exhausted Buddha.

He is joining the party: no longer in my arms all the time, at teatime I put a cushion behind him and prop him up in the high chair. Dash and Evangeline are a circus around him, and he is mesmerized by them. Dolly is long-legged and lovely, a goddess suddenly appearing in his sightline, and he beams when he sees her, always. He has started staring hard at anything the children are eating, so I give him small slices of banana or pieces of broccoli, boiled so soft it is disintegrating.

'Disgusting!' shouts Dash, shoving his plate away with both hands, as Lester pincers the green vegetable into his hand and it makes its way in the general direction of his face.

Very occasionally, I can see Lester as separate from me, but only for tiny chinks of time, like pieces of broken mirror I have found on the floor when I'm throwing toys into the play-box. Sometimes, in those chinks of time, I start to think of Pete a bit more. And when I have the space to think of him, it makes me miss him, because there are so many of us in this marriage.

In bed I roll over in the thin grey light, just before dawn, feeling tiny sharp nails, like the pain of standing on seashells, grasping at the soft area of my breast. Lester lies between us, and in the darkness he latches on, nestling and snuffling. I'm lying beside Pete but it's like there is a piglet between us. Milk soaks the front of my T-shirt. Later a breast pad falls from my bra, and Pete treads on it when he gets up to find some space in another bed in the house, too desperate for rest.

Outside the house, the Indian summer is a vanished mirage of distant memory. When Dolly and Jimmy leave the house in the morning to catch the school bus, there is frost spiking the grass; I have to remind Dolly three times to wear a proper coat. The days are getting shorter: it's still dark as I slop milk and cereal into bowls at breakfast time, and then it's dark again by the time we sit down together for supper.

The darkness and cold outside make the days more exhausting, as if the past months have built up a bank of fatigue, sitting like lead inside me that I must carry with me wherever I go. I am always hungry, consuming pints of milk and jam sandwiches, handfuls of any kind of biscuit I can find, a banana, a plate of pasta and then another pint of milk. Clean eating passes me by: a handful of pumpkin seeds, an oatcake and plain yogurt won't touch the sides. Lying very still at dawn, with the sound of Pete breathing beside me, and Lester feeding, I try to remember how my marriage fits together in between the children.

There is just so little space.

Desire, though, is returning. The assault of childbirth has subsided. I have stopped bleeding, and my stitches are now just a nub of scar tissue. Sex is possible, but sometimes it feels like a function I have to perform. Before I had this baby, I liked sex that pinned me down. I wanted to submit, to be dominated, because this was the thing that made me feel complete. Now, I don't like the feeling of his chest and dark chest hair pressed against my heavy leaking breasts. At the moment my breasts must go nowhere near his mouth. I feel faintly bovine, mooing with exhaustion when Lester wakes in the night.

Often, when I am upstairs feeding Lester late at night, I can hear Pete watching *Newsnight* downstairs. I expect his relationship with Emily Maitlis is more rewarding than the one I can offer. It's certainly more intense.

I feel we might forget one another.

The children come between us at every possible opportunity. Pete has been away every week for the past month so the mothering I've been doing has been front line, often lonely. I see more of Pavel, chat with him more, share more of what the children are up to, than I do with Pete. Even when he is at home at the weekend, it's almost impossible to have a conversation, interrupted incessantly by children swinging from his arms like comedy bananas. We communicate in fragments, as if Samuel Beckett wrote our parts, exchanging fag ends of sentences we never finish. The children chatter away to him all the time, and I am pushed aside like a silenced scullery maid whose role it is to wipe surfaces, find shoes and carry coats.

I miss the people we were together, before we became carers. I'm never ashamed of who I am in front of him, even when I'm angry and hateful with exhaustion, and I crave more of him. Sex is the place we can find one another again. I never have to pretend. I love him more than I thought it possible to love anyone.

Sex is also the opposite of motherhood. As a mother I have to pretend to be the person I really am not: patient, hygienic, gentle, interested in other people's children, good at craft, moderate, rarely anxious, never depressed. When I have sex I can forget all that control and be something different, unembarrassed and lustful, like an animal, but also absolutely human in a dark and disgusting way. It's easier than anything else I know how to do.

I am not so comfortable with all the ways my body functions. I hate it when another person farts in front of me. I don't even like writing that word. There's also no way in the world I'd ever take a crap in front of Pete, but I feel completely at home when he comes on my face. I also like it when he splays me right open so that he can see the most intimate part of me, and my body is his and doesn't belong to mothering any more.

Apart from sex, almost everything we do together is about us as a mother and a father. Sometimes I think I must become someone else through sex so that I don't feel as though I am betraying my children. Sex necessarily involves shutting them out of my mind and my space completely. One of the best things I have done to improve the sex we have, far beyond vibrators and paddles and underwear or even that harness that ties me up, is to put a lock on the inside of our bedroom door. It frees us from cowering under the duvet listening out for small feet. It's hard enough trying to have sex when you are parents without worrying about what will happen if your child walks in while you are kneeling at his father's cock.

When your children are small you regularly feel tired, bored and distracted, which isn't a lustful feeling. And apart from when I'm working, I rarely shut them out of my life. But when I'm thinking about having sex I want them as far away from me as possible. I want to climb right inside sex when it happens. I am greedy. If I could I'd melt my skin and cells and mix them with Pete's while we're having sex. Maybe that's what his come on my face is really making me feel: the relief of being like liquid.

The Obamas were the first people to publicly talk about 'date night'. They might have been running America but they were also parents who seemed to be able to create a sense of marriage and parenthood as something hot and desirable. In interviews, they made date night seem like something any of us could achieve with a satin cocktail dress and a good restaurant. In the real world, that's an unfinished bottle of wine left by the washing-up and an argument about who should go and settle the baby when he wakes at quarter to midnight. If we're lucky, we snatch twenty minutes to drive to the shop to buy milk late at night with Lester, who hasn't settled, in the back of the car. A child is always between us.

Once I've got Dash and Evangeline to bed, I'd like to lie in a dark and silent room, where no one can find me, but instead I try to portion out some energy to Jimmy and Dolly, to chat, to connect in some way.

I find I crave Dolly's company, and her approval. She is changing, quickly but imperceptibly, the small girl she was slipping away. She doesn't realize how lovely she is. Sometimes I run her a bath, and she undresses in front of me. As she clambers in, her brown hair fraying around her face in the water, her whole body looks smooth and completely perfect in a way mine never will again.

Occasionally I catch a glimpse of her watching her reflection in a mirror, with a different kind of poise and power emerging as her features grow stronger, her sense of who she is becoming more marked. She has started borrowing my shoes, too, trying my mascara, and in the evening, after Dash and Evangeline are asleep, she comes to lie on my bed. Then our conversation meanders to new places, to friendships, to the things she's dreaming of and the things that make her scared. She shows me something a friend has posted on social media, and tries to explain to me how to use Snapchat. It remains a mystery.

Watching her changing is extraordinary. This is the little girl who did not walk or talk until she was almost two. As she grows, I feel myself shedding some of the concern I have had for her. The delight she brought with her funny eccentricities crystallized into a hard nub of anxiety when she was six or seven and struggling to manage the basic letter formations to write her name, or read very simple words. As much as I coached myself to stay calm, to believe in her, and to just continue to love her, I worried incessantly about her. She went to a specialist dyslexia school for a couple of years, and while they helped her learn to read, I was shocked when one teacher told me she might not manage mainstream school but would instead need to stay at a specialist school.

'How can they say that about her? She's eight! How can they know where she'll be when she's twelve, or thirteen, or eighteen?' I ranted to Pete. I was furious that anyone could underestimate her, but perhaps I also didn't want to voice my real fears. Maybe she would not cope with normal school. Maybe the teacher was right, and I should lower my expectations for her.

Now, as she lies on the bed beside me, I wish I could reach back into time and wipe those anxieties away. Dolly's path isn't normal; she has a dyslexic brain, and the way she expresses her thoughts is sometimes back to front or upside down. But she can read, and her upside-down thoughts often surprise me because they are so original and emotionally connected.

And being with Dolly is enchanting. She's funny and intuitive, quite unlike anyone else I know. When she was a tiny newborn baby I took some photographs of her with a rosebud in her cot, because that's exactly what she was like. I'm lucky to be her mother and she has taught me that allowing your child to truly be themself, rather than imposing an idea of the person they should or might be, is one of the most important lessons to learn as a parent.

We have not experienced the mother–daughter teenage storms I was expecting; I am lucky – she is sweet and loving, always kind, and way more competent with the younger children than I am most of the time.

One evening, Dolly and I make a plan for her to catch the bus into Oxford, to meet her cousin. I am reluctant to let her go, even though she has a phone, and her cousin will meet her. But this first trip into the world without me scares me, as much as I know it's what she needs. She texts me from the bus and we exchange a handful of chatty notes about what she and her cousin will do together. She texts me again as the bus is coming into Oxford – *Nearly there mum love you* – and I ask her to message me when she meets her cousin. But then her phone goes silent. I call and message – *Have you arrived my love?* Twenty minutes pass; I speak with her cousin. A bus has come and gone, but Dolly wasn't on it. Thirty minutes, and suddenly I'm gasping. I gave Jimmy freedom much earlier than Dolly; we lived in Oxford when he was still in primary school and he often walked there alone. But I'm more protective of Dolly, my sweet girl. Standing in the

kitchen at home, frantically texting her again, I'm curs-
ing myself. Was she too young to make this trip alone?
How can I have let her get on a bus into a city without
really understanding the trip? Dash and Evangeline
paw at me as I pace around, my mind galloping on.
She's been picked up, or gone off with someone. A
man has taken her, my mind shrieks at me, and I
imagine her, walking away from me to a place of great
danger that she cannot see. I think of bundling all the
children into the car, to start driving around laybys on
the ring road to try to find her, my mind racing, racing,
out of control.

My phone pings. *Been in Top Shop. Going for a burger.*
A palpable sense of relief floods through me. Of course
she is fine! She is fine! There was nothing to worry
about!

When Jimmy and Dolly were small, I felt the most
important thing I could give them was my presence. As
a single mother supporting them alone I had to work
hard, and that often took me away from them, but
when the work was done I tried my best to give them
a sense I was really there for them. It was something I
could do that helped me feel connected to my mother,
too. When I was a child, I never questioned the idea
that Mum would be there for me, always. There was an
absolute solidity to her love; it didn't depend on her
mood, but was constant. She must have felt bored and
angry and frustrated at times, and trapped in the kitchen
at home, but if she did, she dealt with it by spending
time outdoors, in the garden planting roses and fruit
trees, or riding her horse.

I continued to crave that sense of my mum's presence throughout my teenage life. I didn't split with her, in the way teenage mothers and daughters are supposed to, although she wasn't that interested in things teenagers like. She didn't show me how to wear mascara, and I think she imagined lip salve and Chanel No. 5 were the only cosmetics worth bothering with. She rarely took me clothes shopping, but was absolutely always there for me, giving me a sense that mothering was a deep joy, and that a baby was the start of a sort of love affair which never really ended. I thought that her love and presence would never end. But it did, when I was sixteen: brain damage from her accident perpetually locking her into a world where she could not communicate. I was thirty-nine when she died, so all the mothering I have done has been without a mother present. And I feel I've been mothering small children for ever; but mothering teenagers, I realize, is new territory. My mother love for the babies is learned, absolutely, from my mother. I try to love them in the way she loved me, absolutely, expansively, and to wrap them in a complete sense of love, and the security that comes with that. Conjuring up happy days for them, with picnics on the bedroom floor, or making dens in the garden, or sitting with them under warm lamplight to read Beatrix Potter are things I can do from the bank of my memory. Being a mother to teenagers isn't familiar like this. I wasn't mothered at all after sixteen. And as I navigate this path with my own teenagers I feel I'm heading into a wilderness. I don't know where the traps and wild animals will be, or how to escape them when they appear.

But while they are small I want my children to bear witness to some of the things I remember from Mum which I hold like the precious shards of childhood: running barefoot across frost on the lawn, walking down an empty road under a moonlit sky, the sting of fizzy-cola-bottle sweets in my cheek just as supper was on the table, the warm, comforting smell of the kitchen when Mum was there. None of these things are dramatic or difficult or expensive to achieve. I'm not talking about a five-star family trip to Disney World or a bed shaped like a racing car. What I want is to give them a feeling of confirmed security and love within a childhood that's steeped in its own special and peculiar colour. I want them to be able to take that memory out, later, when life gets difficult, to help show them the way through.

The children are full of joy; they laugh and skip around me, occupied by tricks and games. But the responsibility to create happy childhoods for them can feel solemn, even though what I want for them is, simply, that joy. Most of all, though, I hope that they will remember the conversations we have had as we step in and out of one another's lives, and that they will remember me as being there for them. And I want them to always be able to communicate with me. The shadow of my mother's brain damage that prevented her speaking is always there. Sometimes I want to shake Jimmy when he's angry with me, sullenly cooking his third fried breakfast of the day, and shout at him: Do you have any idea what being a teenager with no mother is like? The inheritance of loss is intense.

And what I definitely want to try to do is survive for my children. Occasionally I get scared that some force will inexorably take me away from them, repeating my own experience of being a daughter. I'm alone in the car, and I imagine myself driving into the back of a lorry, or off the edge of a bridge. Sometimes it feels as if I'm constantly running away from this sense of loss, trying too hard to shore up my children's lives against it.

In the dark tunnel, there are tiny gaps appearing when Lester doesn't need me. Now Pavel can take him to a baby group in the mornings when Dash is at pre-school, so I have an hour and a half alone.

One morning, pushing Lester in his buggy down to Evangeline's school gate as she skips away in front, golden hair swinging, the everlasting sprite, and Dash walking beside me clutching the edge of the buggy, another mother, smiling broadly with a frowning baby strapped to her front, stops to peer at Lester inside.

'Hello, Lester! You loved Rhyme Time last week, didn't you! Trying to clap and everything, bless him,' she says, grinning at Lester as if he understands what she is talking about.

I smile and laugh, leaning over to give his tummy, wrapped up in a knitted blanket, a little squeeze, but it makes me feel a bit bad. Maternal guilt at having any time off is strong. I'm the one who should have been taking him to Rhyme Time, even though that hour and a half was the time I'd used to try and put my head back together after the pixilation of the previous twenty-three hours. I'd vanished with my laptop to a cafe. I have work to do, but I can also waste every minute of the short time I have in which to write scrolling through fake-news websites, reading about other people's arguments on Facebook or following threads about the best way to peel garlic on Twitter.

The pop-up ads online confuse me but also keep me coming back. They offer me sheepskin slippers, a holiday cottage in the Lake District, and tell me that Russian Beauties are waiting for me. This seems highly unlikely. But I like the thought of them talking to one another quietly in a language I don't understand, in the threadbare room of a remote cottage somewhere, waiting for me.

It is mid-morning, and I'm at a desk in the sitting room, writing at my computer, when Pete calls me from New York, where he's working. He wants to FaceTime. It's exciting. Lester is sleeping in his cot and Dash is playing trains with Pavel in the kitchen.

Suddenly, Pete's face is in the palm of my hand, on my phone. It's shockingly intimate, the closest I've come to holding anything of Pete in the past month.

Beautifully illuminated on the little screen, he shimmers with light and he's all smiles when he sees me appear. From the edge of the screen I can see the grey plastic box of a taxi he's travelling in, a pavement moving beyond view. Outside the screen, beyond reach, are people and skyscrapers and the glitter of urban life moving very quickly, as if in a film.

'Yes, I'm in a taxi,' he says when I ask, as though it's obvious, looking away and then back at me, smiling quickly, his mind probably darting to something more pressing.

In the room next door I hear Dash shouting and a door banging, a return to domesticity after a glimpse of New York. I readjust my face in an attempt to smooth the creases on my forehead so that I look nicer. I want to look less like a wife, less like a mother. The image of the street around Pete is moving more quickly now, and mine is standing still.

I imagine him moving all day, walking into and through big, important conference rooms and board-rooms. I imagine what it feels like to do business. Cards handed out, fast adult conversations driven by urgency and purpose. They have energy and are going some-where. It makes me miss him desperately.

When I first fell in love with Pete, but before we were sleeping together, I thought about sex with him a lot. I liked his voice and the shape of his mouth; I liked the smell of him so much that I wanted to snort him like a drug. I didn't want to just sleep with him, or be with him in a vague, sociable way, but I wanted to become a part of him. I also thought he was quite a different person to the man he really is. I thought I'd have to pretend to him I was someone who did not fall in love, and who did not get attached, because I thought that was how he might be with me.

I wanted to have sex with him so much I couldn't think of anything else most days, but I told myself not to get bound up with him. I didn't think I could trust him. One day, early on, he told me his work involved being abroad a lot. I knew the conferences he went to were important, but I also thought that once the work was done some of the men and women would go out together and later have sex. When he told me about an interesting woman he met who worked in marine biology, I imagined he was having sex with her too, because it was the only thing I really wanted to do with him, even when he was talking to me about ocean pollution.

Seeing Pete on my FaceTime, looking so very adult, reminds me of this way I thought of him when we first met, before we did all this caring together. I want to tell him something interesting about my day: Evangeline has ballet later, we almost missed the school bus, and I've sat at my computer. I've wondered if I could give them rice and sausages for supper again, and I've googled recipes for sausage casserole and then given up because we don't have most of the ingredients. I managed to get to the chemist before it shut for lunch to buy nit lotion.

And then I imagine Manhattan girls in tight black suits wearing high-heeled shoes with red soles. A flick book in my mind I can't control runs through films like *Wolf of Wall Street* or *Basic Instinct*: hot, horny cartoon women and men in stressful business situations that they then take out on one another's bodies. My mind flicks between my palm, where I'm holding Pete, and my computer screen open on the desk in front of me where I had been writing about my thoughts. The two screens compete, confusing me, and now I see a slight, skinny girl with shiny straight brown hair kneeling at his feet, and his hand is cupped around the back of her head, fingers laced through her hair, pushing her head backwards and forwards.

'Clover? Did it go OK?' Pete's voice cuts through my imaginings. I look back at the tiny moving image of

myself in the corner of the screen. Behind me there is
the new wallpaper in the sitting room we took so long
to choose because I was so tired from breastfeeding,
and I notice my roots badly need dyeing and my blonde
hair looks too yellow.

'The kids' class, did it go OK?' he asks.

'Yes, it was fine, they're all fine,' I say, because I don't
actually know which class he's talking about, and now
I don't want to ask.

This time I don't tell him about Dash screaming at
me at five this morning to play a train cartoon on my
phone, the dentist appointment I forgot or shrinking
my favourite jersey in the washing machine. Those
were the most dramatic things that happened to me
this week.

Pete wants to tell me about a meeting because it
went well and I like it that he wants to share that with
me, but I keep thinking of the girl I might be, kneeling
in a hotel room with his cock in my mouth.

Then I feel a wetness on my T-shirt. In an upstairs
bedroom Lester cries and my body responds, leaking
milk.

Pete's face freezes, his mouth in a perfect O, as the
connection comes and goes, and we see one another in
slow motion but we can't hear anything the other is
saying.

In the community centre around me, sealed from the
energy of cars passing on the road outside, mothers sit
and wait. Mothers do this a lot.

From 3 p.m. every weekday there are millions of
women waiting in community centres, beside swimming

pools, on the edge of football pitches, in traffic jams. We cook supper then we wait for the children we've called to come to the table to eat. We squeeze toothpaste on to a brush and wait while the child clamps his or her jaw shut. We sit on the edges of beds, waiting, stroking a stray strand of hair flat until our daughters sleep deeply enough that they won't notice we've gone. We wait and we wait until our children do what we tell them, and then they are grown and we are older. The wait I find hardest is the sweaty, noisy one beside the swimming pool. Then, I try to think of the pleasure Evangeline will get diving into the sea or swimming across a river. Another part of me feels as though my brain is draining out of my heel through the verruca-covered drains. As a mother I am living a life that is not, for much of the time, mine.

So I am experienced at waiting, but today, waiting in the community centre for Evangeline to start and then finish ballet, I am feeling absolutely flattened by it. I have left Lester and Dash with Pavel, giving myself a whole hour away to drive Evangeline to her class, which she loves and is good at, which will give me thirty minutes with myself, while she is dancing.

I watch her in the mirror as we drive. She has a doll on her lap that she's undressed. There's blue felt-tip-pen scribble on the doll's face, but the doll looks patient as Evangeline pulls a bright pink plastic comb through her nylon hair. Beyond her main goal of persuading me to get her a pet, Evangeline tends to her plastic dolls with a degree of care and attention that puts me to shame. They are her children, who must be fed and changed several times a day.

'Mum, you've put the shopping on top of your granddaughter!' she chides me when I put a bag of shopping on top of a doll in the back of the car by accident. She will never settle to bed until all the dolls are tucked in. She finds tiny corners for them, on the sofa in her room, in an old shoebox, under the covers of her bed. When I walk around the house at night switching out lights, tiny plastic faces stare up at me, eyes wide open, as though they're reproaching me, patiently biding their time until their real mother, Evangeline, comes back.

'I'm thinking of opening a cafe,' she informs me from the back of the car. 'Yes, a cafe selling Fanta to run beside my pet shop. That's what I want to do when I'm older. Be a doctor or have a cafe and a pet shop. And be a mum. I really want to be a mum like you.' She pauses, smiling at me as though she is about to ask me a favour. 'Do you think a pet fish would be possible, if we can't get the rabbits yet? Sardines, maybe? Would that be a good idea? Mum, did you also know that when cats close their eyes they are actually making a kiss. But only when they close their eyes slowly. It's actually a secret kiss.'

She chatters on with little surprises – 'Oh, I wish it was pancake day!' – as I park the car, slipping her small, hot hand into mine as we walk across the car park, but when we go into the community centre, full of children, her voice quietens. I feel her pressing herself against me, before we settle at a low table in the cafe and I start pulling her ballet kit on to her soft limbs, rolling little pink socks on to her feet, smoothing them up her perfect legs, sliding her ballet shoes on, pulling a brush in a futile way through her blonde tangles as she pulls away from me, now ready.

'I'm fine, Mum. It's brushed,' she says, skipping off to a far room for her lesson. She is completely perfect, almost shimmering, lovely and lively. As I watch her vanishing into the room, I wonder how something so perfect can have come from me.

The mothers in the community centre sit facing one another on low grey sofas. They wear stretchy clothes coloured like autumn, plum and dark orange and maroon and brown. The heat and airlessness of the room feels sludgy, but they talk brightly, their voices bouncing off one another, laughing as they shake their heads remembering a silly little thing he did at bathtime last night. It's intimate, but makes me feel as though my head is wrapped in clingfilm. I want to get out.

I can't, of course. Waiting for Evangeline, I have twenty-eight minutes to myself in which to think about my work. I pull out a notebook and start making a list of projects I could pitch to editors. At the table beside me, two women are discussing half-term holidays and their conversation slides along to work. One of them is thinking of returning to work now that both her children are in school full-time and she's seen an opening for staff in a nearby supermarket.

'I mean the money's not great, barely above the minimum wage, but it's the benefits I'm interested in really.'

'Don't you get a healthy discount at John Lewis when you work in Waitrose?'

'Yes, it's twenty-five per cent off. That could come in very handy at Christmas.' She is relacing her daughter's shoes. 'And finding part-time work isn't easy. I want to be there as much as I can for the children but I haven't been in any kind of full-time work for six years now because of the kids.'

'What did you do before?' the other woman asks. 'Before children, I mean?'

'Oh, I was a molecular scientist,' she says quickly.

They are both quiet for a moment. The scientist folds a small T-shirt her daughter has left on the floor at her feet.

'Oh, look at that. They're selling the flapjacks off half price,' her new friend says.

'Perhaps they've passed their sell-by date,' replies the molecular scientist. 'But still. She'll be hungry when she comes out.'

Leaning up against the wall near them, a woman is sitting on the floor, rolling a football between her two sons. I can see the tracing of a tattoo on the top of her arm, faded and spidery, as if in the past it might have taken her to a place of adventure. There was a wild life for her, once. I put my notebook down and finish my tea, which is cold now.

Evangeline skips back into view and my heart clenches with guilt at my boredom and claustrophobia, as if she might be able to see these feelings hanging around me.

As I lift her on to my lap to pull her ballet socks from her, I bury my face in the back of her neck. Now what I feel, more than anything, is how I love her: so intensely that tears rise inside me. She is so tender, this perfect girl.

'How can I tell you how much I love you?' she whispers to me. 'Mum, I love you so much. I love you always. I just can't tell you how much I love you.'

It rains all weekend in sheets that do not stop. We have to dart from the car to the house. Everyone is drenched. The children bounce off the walls and I walk around with Lester watching them, hanging from my arm. Pete is back for the weekend and, because of the rain, we take the children out for lunch in a pub, just to leave the house. Pens and colouring pencils replace forks and napkins, which are folded up to make blankets for a doll, a tunnel for a train, tiny duvets for sleeping Sylvanians, who nestle beneath a salt shaker. It's like running an oversubscribed craft workshop, rather than an enjoyable family experience.

Later, much later, when the children are asleep, we lie in bed, facing one another. At first being naked, touching each other's bodies, is almost embarrassing. That makes me feel turned on, too. It's like having sex with a stranger, but a stranger I desire as much as I want Pete, which is more than anyone I've ever met. Sometimes, when we're having sex, he covers my eyes, so I can imagine he's having sex with someone different. I only want him but sometimes I like thinking about him with someone else, to feel the pain and pleasure of it. Sex enables me to become the woman who doesn't worry about whether everyone has their coats for school or their homework has been done. I can't really do anything about the kids when my wrists are pinned to the bed, and my face is forced into a pillow. Sex like that takes you to different places, like suddenly being on very strong drugs.

After, there is the unfamiliar, wet reassurance of spunk on the sheets. Something fragmented in me feels, for a moment, as if it's put back together.

Then, from the next room, Lester starts crying.

6

Working Away

For much of the winter that Lester spends learning how to sit up, to laugh, to eat, to sleep, to walk in small loops around the house, I'm trying to keep my head together. Before they leave for school, Dash and Evangeline create chaos, but when I am alone with Lester, I try to still myself to his pace.

I spread a blanket on the floor, arranging pillows in a semi-circle like a soft-play version of an AA meeting. Lester sits propped up in the middle, grabbing at the coloured bricks or large plastic pieces of Lego I hastily scatter in front of him in a distracted maternal offering. I try not to bundle him through the moments before his rest, even though I know that the faster I do it, the more time I'll have in front of my laptop to make my thoughts my own again, writing small snatches of words that will form my work.

I read *Where's Spot?* and *Where the Wild Things Are* and *Are You My Mummy?* hundreds of times, propping Lester up on my lap as I turn the pages while deeply inhaling that sweet, sweet smell of the top of his baby's head. When I lay him down to change him, I see myself reflected in his eyeballs. As I put him down into his cot, he just about manages to smile back at me through half-closed eyes, sleepy with breast milk. The beauty and charm of his existence pierce the isolation of domestic life.

I go back downstairs and empty the cup of tea I made an hour earlier, where a cold milky scum has formed on the top. I open my computer to try and write, until the urgency of the washing machine bleeping its finished load overtakes me, and I start wandering around the house again, picking up discarded clothes, carting toys back upstairs to the children's bedroom, opening curtains which have blocked out the light since the rush of the morning.

Often I have to stare at the screen for a very long time, trying to piece together the jumble in my mind, before I can make thoughts my own again. What appears on a Word document I closed the night before might be written in Arabic, or Urdu. I barely recognize my own ideas. When this happens, I turn to social media and gossip sites to distract me from the panic. I could have read all of the work of Tolstoy, Dickens, Dostoevsky and the Brontës and still have weeks to spare in the time I've spent with my brain dribbling out of my ears on Instagram. I blame my scrambled brain on motherhood. But it could equally easily be my dopamine addiction.

I think of T. S. Eliot. For some of his life, he worked in a bank, moving pieces of paper around, but he also felt and wrote *The Waste Land*. He wrote 'Journey of the Magi', which I read to Dash and Evangeline at bedtime when I cannot face another picture book. I think they're oblivious to the words as they sit up in bed, playing with the trains and plastic horses tangled up in their duvets, until one of them interrupts to ask me what alien gods look like.

Thinking about T. S. Eliot, I feel less bad about monotony. I know that the mundane can mask an overwhelmingly meaningful experience, something I remind myself as I try to fold elasticated sheets or make a cheese sauce stretch to cover both cauliflower cheese and lasagne for the freezer, and in particular when scraping toothpaste from the inside of the sink.

Often I hear my voice telling me this in my own head as I move around the house, hanging wet washing over radiators, or crawling under the kitchen table to pick up grains of rice, grated cheese and slices of apple that have been sucked and then spat out. Many hours of the day are spent with Lester on my hip or on my shoulder, his head bobbing up and down as I walk from room to room, wondering if I actually feel happy, clearing toys, sorting clothes, finding shoes, filling book bags.

And when I sit down, Lester sits on my lap, where I pull him closer in to me, running my hand over the back of his head where his curls fit in the nape of his neck, kissing his soft skin as he leans in towards me, gently patting me with his starfish hand. Although Lester won't remember any of these long days we had together, of me mothering him when he is so small, I hope I am imprinting into him a sense of having been loved. When we sit quietly together and he presses his small shoulders against me, I know he feels something good, like comfort or ease or even happiness, even if he won't remember it. This is all I need to achieve.

Sometimes I think about cave women. I would like to understand what they did after their babies were born. How soon after birth did they start sweeping the cave? How soon did they go back hunting? Did the walls of the cave start feeling darker and closer when their babies were small? Did they crave the silent relief of killing an animal to eat or feeling wet earth under their feet?

As Lester grows, the force field of new motherhood keeping me separate from much of the adult world dissolves. The light looks sharper and the colours of the world more primary. The special kind of blessing his arrival bestowed on our home meant that for a while time didn't exactly stop, but it certainly became a lot less pressing. Bill, emails, even entire friends lose their relevance when the central purpose of your life is to support another being much, much more vulnerable than yourself.

But by six months Lester is sitting up in his high chair. When I lay him on his tummy on the bedroom floor, he can push himself up, rocking backwards and forwards, preparing to propel himself into the world. Soon, he will stand up on Pete's lap while clasping his fingers, and drool with excitement when he gets hold of car keys, mobile phones or the purple plastic lighter Jimmy leaves out on the kitchen table.

I still feed him, mostly at night, because at lunchtime he grasps the spoon I am using to post mashed-up broccoli pasta into his mouth. He smiles and laughs, pointing from his high chair to our dog, Pablo, who waits, devoted, beneath his chair, for the food Lester sprinkles.

'Pabo, Pabo, Pabo,' he later says, swinging his toes and little legs, straining down with his pointed finger to reach Pablo's upturned black nose. Pabo is his first proper word.

As the world comes back into focus I feel a familiar tension between guilt and desire for something else, for something more. My desire to look past my family and back out at the world, to fix my gaze on a distant horizon, tugs at me, insistent, but with it I also feel that familiar silent pressure of guilt. I need to earn money, of course, and there are things I want to do, thoughts I want to have, which don't involve Lester at all, or any of the children. I want to wrestle myself away from them, and try to put away the small, heavy box of guilt I carry when I'm not with them.

One morning I receive an email from someone I had worked with a couple of years before. He says it's so nice to hear I've finally *settled down*. The words jump out at me from the screen like a silly joke. I have a home and family, but nothing about me feels any more settled than it has ever done. The valleys I ride through every day as a mother are as difficult and steep as they were when I was out in the world. If someone could see inside me, they might say: She didn't have a baby and settle down; she had a baby and became extremely disturbed.

If I had had a big accident, or I'd been mugged and had precious things taken from me, I would talk about it. But we don't talk about the things motherhood takes away from us in this way. And the thoughts and freedoms we lose when we become mothers are invisible, because what we gain – the love that defines our relationships with these golden children – is so huge.

In the mornings after I have dropped the children at school, I listen to drive-time radio shows during which cheerful presenters talk with urgency about the nation's commute and the start of the working day. It's all quite unfamiliar. An appointment with the health visitor is a rare punctuation mark in the working week when Lester and I have to leave the house with any sense of urgency. Nobody actually notices or cares if you are late for the mother-and-toddler drop-in session at the community hall.

But in these still days dozens of urgent matters need my attention all of the time. Number one urgent thing is to change the nappy that's now leaking into dark rings at the top of his tights. Number two – to grab him as he reaches for the clothes drying on the rack that threatens to topple over. Three – to remove the end of a saucepan handle that's been left too close to the edge of the kitchen table, which a small hand is straining, straining to reach. Other, sudden moments of urgency happen in my days as a mother, out of nowhere, reminding me danger can erupt into my life at any second. Once I put Lester down on the carpet while I emptied the dishwasher, and a second later his face was purple and his mouth open, with no sound coming from it. I lunged for him and smacked him between his shoulder blades, guddling frantically in his drooling mouth with my fingers, dislodging a small piece of toast. He started breathing again and I continued putting the knives and forks away. A few weeks later, he was lying on the sofa as I stroked his tummy, and when I looked away to reach for my phone, he rolled over. I caught him quickly – motherhood gives you fast reflexes – but if I hadn't he would have slammed his head on the edge of a wooden table.

These moments of mortal urgency happen so fast, and are so frequent, that I slide straight into the next moment – looking for a hairbrush, slicing garlic – and there's never a chance to focus on what might have been. Mothers guard against death and injury several times a day. They are quiet soldiers on the domestic front.

But spending many days alone with my baby reminds me how much I miss being needed to think, rather than to do things. I can make meals, drive children around, supervise homework, fill shopping trolleys. But I need to think, too. Admitting this feels like a betrayal of Lester and all my children in the most primal way: my baby – my beautiful, healthy, funny, sweet, golden baby – is not enough. How can I ever say I need more than this baby?

At the school gate, I smile and try to look happy. When another mum asks me how I am, I lie.

I don't say that I frequently feel crushed, bored, angry and completely fucked off. This mum wouldn't want to hear about it. Nothing actually bad has happened. But at the same time, something important that I liked before has been altered, and something important that was mine has been lost.

Sometimes when I feel myself wandering around with the children and feeling very empty, or yawning a lot, I go out into the garden to pull up thistles from the lawn. They make my hands sting but the pain makes me feel alive. Occasionally, while slicing red peppers for Bolognese, I imagine what it would be like to run the sharp blade of the knife across my palm. The self-control I am exercising is tightly wound around me all of the time. I love my children with my entire heart. When I want to imagine how I would destroy my life, I imagine it without my children. I'm one of the luckiest people alive on the planet today. I have everything that I ever wanted. And yet, I am also howling.

> *Darling, I'm loving seeing pics of your brood on Instagram. I honestly don't know how you do it. And the little one is divine.*
>
> *Any chance you'd be up for an interview? It's with a TV explorer – bit of a heartthrob in fact! And we'd love to have your voice back with us. But no pressure. Only when YOU are ready.*

As I scroll through her email, I hear Yasna's voice, purring at me, above the high-pitched shrieks of Dash and Evangeline as they create a space station with pet-loading area out of a pile of wooden bricks, Lester watching as if to learn.

I met Yasna eleven years ago, on a press trip to Italy. She was desperate for children at the time, and had started IVF. She fell pregnant two months into the process, and now has two sons. Her husband works part-time, and she runs the website for an international lifestyle brand. She spends every day in an office, taking a cab home promptly at six thirty to read to her children before they go to bed. Magic hour, she calls it. She sees her children for ninety minutes every evening.

When she gave birth, she had prepared cue cards, and everything ran like clockwork. She is strong. Once she confided to me that she gave birth at home, without any painkillers.

'Not even gas and air?' I gasped, and she shook her head, laughing.

'Nothing except the power of my mind. It's a powerful muscle.'

Motherhood, she once told me, is what makes her happiest. 'When I'm with my children I am completely content. They are everything for me,' she said. I wonder if she loves it because she is away from her children all day.

I open my computer and reread Yasna's message. I have done bits and pieces of writing since Lester was a few weeks old. Sometimes, I write pieces on my phone while I am feeding him. At least once a week, I field calls from commissioning editors, propping my phone on my shoulder with Lester under one arm, or sit with my back against the bathroom door, trying to ignore Dash's angry little fists pummelling on it so that I can finish a piece of work. I have not, yet, taken a whole day away from Lester in order to go away to work. It's

a liberating thought. I open an email and tell her I'd
love to do the interview.

Mothering is often solitary, but so is the job I do. My
entire working life, apart from disastrous waitressing
jobs or a position I once had teaching English as a foreign language to businessmen, has been spent at my
laptop, writing articles to sell to newspapers and maga-
zines, and then later a book.

When Evangeline was a week and a half old a newspaper editor I wrote for emailed to ask if I'd be free to
do an interview. *We'd love to have you writing for us again,
but we know you've just had a baby. No pressure! xxL.*

It was a cover story, with a pop star, and I knew that
to be asked at all was a big deal. Masses of pressure! It
mattered for my career. Her email arrived when I was
driving home from my sister's. She'd been telling me to
take it easy.

'Don't worry about working, if you can. Leave it, for
a few weeks at least. Give yourself the time. You've got
three children to look after. And yourself, too. Look
after yourself,' she'd said. 'Cut back on all other expenses,
so that you can let work wait for a bit.' I'd had to pull
over on to the verge, because Evangeline was crying in
her baby seat, inhaling air in a screeching noise that
made her sound as though she might turn herself inside
out with hunger. I read through my emails as I fed her,
pressed up against the steering wheel.

No problem, I messaged the editor back. *I'd love to
do it.*

Of course, I had to take Evangeline with me, as I was
breastfeeding and she was tiny. My closest friend Etain

came along as well, walking Evangeline around the lobby of a twinkling London hotel while I sat in an upstairs room with a pop princess dressed all in black lace, who answered my questions as if reading from a script. I knew the only story my editor was actually interested in was why, despite her meteoric career, she had not had children. I picked my way through my questions, while her assistants stepped in and out with ginger tea, but most of the time I was focused on willing my breasts not to start leaking.

I knew that Evangeline might start crying, downstairs in the hotel lobby, and privately I wished I hadn't said yes to the commission. Just getting to the interview, with my newborn baby in tow, had made me feel as though I was walking around with my fists scrunched up in tension. I shouldn't have been in a hotel room with a megastar while my hungry baby was being walked around downstairs by my friend. Asking the megastar why she hadn't had kids when I felt flayed alive by my own felt absurd.

When I drove back home to Oxford, Evangeline screamed all the way until I pulled over and fed her in a service station. I cried the rest of the way, and cried again as I wrote up the interview with my baby spreadeagled across my lap.

This time round, writing the article for Yasna will give me a damn good reason to get some head space away from limpet Lester. I can feel less guilty when I send Lester and Dash off with Pavel to a baby group. The thoughts I have while sitting at my laptop liberate me, and for all of the time I am writing, suddenly I can wrestle my world back within my own personal control. It's much easier than keeping Dash under control.

I work out that if I time my train just right, I can feed Lester at home then get into London, get the interview done, and be back home in six hours. Lester will be sleeping for almost two-thirds of this time, I remind myself when guilt pinches.

'It's fine, all fine. You go, enjoy your time,' says Pavel, pushing me out of the door when the day arrives, but I wish he didn't sound as if he was sending me off to a spa for the day.

Because I don't have much time, it feels as though I'm on a fast and possibly dangerous, slightly clandestine mission. At the train station, I see a sign that reads, 'AVOID SLIPS AND TRIPS. TAKE CARE!' It's so annoying: doesn't the world know I'm out in it for the first time in weeks? To be babied is the last thing I want.

Because out in the wild, everything feels exciting. Walking past a flower stand covered in the bright pops of colourful tulips, roses and lilies is like suddenly taking acid. Even the Brutalist concrete of the train station is exciting. There have been times in the past few months, as I paced around the kitchen as Lester cried at me and clung to me, when the thought of getting into the city, on my own, seemed as distantly impossible as sailing down the Nile.

My interview is to take place in the offices of the explorer's publishing house. The concrete and glass of this building feels equally alien. It makes me sweat, and instantly I have to take my jacket off, even though it's winter, and this causes the cheap rayon shirt I'm wearing (the only one that is both smart and will fit

over my giant breasts) to suddenly become static and
stick to me. I'm flushed and looking obscenely maternal, even though Lester is over a hundred miles away
from me. But he's with me in spirit, tugging at me, all
of the time.

I am told to wait at reception, and through the windows I watch young men and women walking backwards and forwards with computer bags and books.
The girls all wear short dresses and opaque black tights;
their movements are neat and precise. After the white
noise and ceaseless movement and stickiness of home,
the quiet order of the office is almost confusing, the
solemnity of the way everyone walks around, not dashing, darting or screaming as my children do, almost as if
they have recently been bereaved.

The explorer, when he arrives, is cool, in an expen-
sive-looking dishevelled denim jacket. He sends his
female assistant away to pick up lunch for him. When
she returns, he eats fast, hunched over a plastic box of
rice and green vegetables as I ask him questions. He
says he's sorry to do so while we speak, but explains
that because he's on the road a lot he usually feels he is
too busy to eat.

'I don't get a chance to eat hot food at all, sitting down,
or to finish a cup of tea. There's always so much going
on. It's really quite relentless,' he explains, and I find it
curious that that part of our lives sounds so similar.

He tells me about travelling through mountains, or
across deserts, venturing into the wilderness for a living, often with a cameraman. When I ask why he's so
attracted to dangerous lands, he replies that it's prefer-
able to domestic monotony. We laugh. I tell him I have

spent a lot of time in the part of Russia, near Chechnya, he made a TV programme about; he just nods and continues talking about his own experiences in South America.

'Quite something, isn't he?' the publicist says, after he's gone. 'So brave.'

I think of the women in the community centre, waiting for their children, and the distant look of longing of the mother with the faded tattoo. I think of the way she talked with her children, carefully, without getting distracted, as they rolled a ball between them. I think of the molecular scientist going to work in a supermarket in order to be home early for her children, of the brave sacrifices made.

Remembering the breathy thrill I felt when I left the house, the perimetered pleasure of the train journey and the cup of coffee that wasn't sloshed from my hand on to the clean pair of jeans, the newspaper that wasn't ripped and grabbed to be stuffed into a gummy mouth, I try to step back inside that easy feeling of solitary novelty as I walk back through the city to my train. But something is pressing down on me. It's the anxiety of knowing Lester, in some way, will be aware that I'm not with him. My breathing becomes shallow. I close my eyes. I miss myself when I'm with them and I miss them when I'm away from them. It never stops.

Alone in the city, I feel just as claustrophobic as I have on the long days spent in the kitchen with Lester and Dash as my only company. If I think too much about it, I feel giddy with claustrophobia. I cannot tell who I am any more. On the tube I have to stop myself staring at other women. Opposite me is a girl with curly black hair, wearing a mid-calf printed skirt, white pumps and a leather jacket. She has the smooth, easy look of a girl who is not thinking about where she can buy mouse ears for a costume for World Book Day, or whether she's remembered the ingredients for cheese puffs for her daughter's DT class. She looks way more self-contained than that.

The mothers are easy to identify. They have a look of strain – imperceptible to most people but absolutely obvious to other mothers – that pulses, insistent, behind their eye sockets. They stare more, at their watches, at their phones, because their time doesn't belong to them, and their clothes and accessories – bags and boots – are a little more thrashed. The women who are mothers look as I feel, as though they inhabit skins which don't belong to them, since they carry little pieces of their children wherever they are.

In London, hours away from the children, I inhabit five skins and not one of them is mine.

At Paddington Station I crane at the boards, and with twelve minutes until my train leaves, I go to WHSmith. I feel I need to buy the children something as a small token of apology for the fact that I've been away. I buy postcards of Paddington Bear for Dash, a unicorn pencil for Evangeline, a notebook with a black cover and hot-pink pages for Dolly. Some conciliatory chocolate for Jimmy.

Hurrying back along the platform to catch the train, I have to stop myself holding on to my breasts, which now feel like small tankers, heavy with the weight of milk gathering. They are hot and hard, and I'm so desperate to release the mounting pressure I almost want to plead with the mother at the far end of the carriage. She has a toddler in a buggy and I could help to stop him crying for his bottle if she'd just let me use him to empty my breasts.

To distract myself I scroll through photos Pavel has sent me of Dash, sitting on a swing, and Lester, looking small and confused, staring up from his buggy in the cold park. I want to look at the pictures but they also make me so upset I fear that I have tears gathering. Do my sons feel my absence? They have been to a local museum and Dash is dressed up, wearing a peaked cap and smiling broadly into the camera, pleased with himself. But he also looks alone. Maybe this is a good thing. This is what he will have to do: go out, go away from me and Pete, into life.

I put the phone face down on the train table in front of me. A woman in the seat opposite is drinking a small bottle of white wine from a plastic glass she bought from the buffet trolley. I want to vanish into the glass.

Beside me, across the aisle, three people are having a conversation about a man who had been told off for returning to his mother's house late, drunk, in the middle of the night.

'No matter how old you are, your mum is your mum,' the woman tells another woman sitting opposite her, and the woman nods, pulling her hand out of a packet of crisps she's sharing with the man beside her. He chuckles, and says, 'Yeah, but women are mad.' They all laugh.

Then the first woman says, 'But women forgive everything. They have to, don't they, 'specially mums.

Think what your mum had to forgive you, Rich.' She looks up through her fringe at the man opposite, and none of them laugh this time.

At Slough, a mother and her small daughter work their way through the carriage and settle in the seat opposite me. Quickly the mother pulls a colouring pad and a handful of felt-tips from her bag. Her handbag is missing a buckle, and her hair is frizzy. The child whispers something to her, and the mother fishes out a plastic bag with some biscuits in it. The little girl leans into her mother, while pulling her colouring closer to her. Instinctively, the woman reaches up, stroking the child's auburn hair. The girl shuts her eyes slowly, like the cat Evangeline told me about, doing a secret kiss.

'Muuuuummmmmmmeeeeeeeee!' scream Dash and Evangeline. 'She's back, she's back, she's here!' I am a returning celebrity and they are almost turning themselves inside out with excitement, a whirlwind of bright eyes, bright skin, shiny hair, rich and simple joy bouncing off them as they hurl themselves at me when I get out of my car. Dash opens his arms to launch himself at me with the same look of wild abandon on his face as when he throws himself into a swimming pool. Evangeline springs into me, wrapping her arms and legs around me and clinging on so tight, melding us back together. Dash's words come tumbling out, trying to impart his delight at a train he took from playgroup, the fact that Jake, who is younger than him (an important detail), stole his rice cake but he didn't mind, that he sang to Lester when he was crying at lunchtime, and could he sleep in my bed? Dolly rushes into the kitchen to hug me as well. She has grown a full inch since I left this morning.

Their love is extraordinary. It is dazzling. I am completely unworthy. At this moment, I never want to be away from them again, even for an afternoon, even for a moment.

I start spending longer away from Lester: a few hours at my computer to write each day, more afternoons in London for work and a day speaking at a literary festival. I glug down the time away, but it takes planning. Pavel becomes a regular at baby groups. He needs to be shown, again, how to heat up the stew I'd prepared before I left, and that the potatoes have to be cooked and mashed, so they're ready to warm up.

The work and time away is liberating. I start to see myself as someone separate from my family. But my thoughts return to them all the time. I cannot get away from them. I start writing about them.

Once, I travel east for five hours, to an event in a bookshop in Suffolk. The Fens slink past, winter light dipping on power lines and back gardens. I am now miles and miles from home. Sometimes the signal goes on my phone, but in between there are messages from the children. Mostly these are about food.

Can we cook the garlic bread in freezer?
Do you know if we have my ingredients for cooking tomorrow?
I need PE kit do you know where it is?
What time are you home?
Where are the sausages?

Is there chocolate somewhere?
When are you home?
Will you be home soon?

I am in Suffolk to talk about *The Wild Other*, the book I wrote before Lester was born. The room is full of adults, and it's a novelty to talk for an hour without anyone needing me to take them to the loo or asking me to find their art homework.

'Your book, I loved it,' says a man at my arm as I'm getting ready to walk to the hotel in the town where I'm staying. He tips his head to one side as he speaks, his hair falling slightly over his eyes. I feel myself smiling and heat in my face. He grasps my hand. 'I wanted to tell you how much I love your writing and the way you express yourself.' He's a writer, too, he says, and he holds a copy of my book as if it's something really important. He repeats that he really, really loved it. He keeps eye contact and I like this feeling of his hot attention. Suddenly I realize I recognize him from an interview in a Sunday paper, and had heard him on a podcast a few weeks before. He also has a book out. When he asks me if I want to get a drink in the pub across from the bookshop, I hesitate for a moment at the thought of sitting in a bar with a man who loves what I have to say so much, who is not Pete. The idea of it seems distant, like remembering a holiday where you were very happy from a long time ago. I pause, just for a moment, trying to work out if he's alone, or with a friend, a girlfriend. There's no one else left, apart from the lady who runs the bookshop, moving around in a back room, switching off lights. Not to go out with him would suggest I was guilty in some way. I don't feel guilty. Or not *that* guilty – yet. He's asking me to have a drink. He's not asking me to sleep with him, even if he does have this deep, unbroken way of looking at me, like he wants something I have.

The pub smells of fried food but it's cosy, with twinkling yellow lights and a fire in the corner, and at first we sit, separated by a small table, glasses of wine between us. After he returns from the bar again, he pulls his chair around, so that our knees are pressed together. He wants to talk about my book and the stories in it, and also tell me about the new thing he's working on.

There is something in the way he talks that's more pressing than the way anyone has spoken to me for a while. He makes a joke and I laugh too loudly: I am enjoying myself. I feel very wide awake, and my voice sounds different, as if I can hear it from the outside talking about myself as someone separate from home, separate from my family. He uses my name all the time. He only sees me as Clover.

His most recent book is about danger and resilience. He says he likes taking risks, and he shifts forward in his chair, putting his hand over mine, squeezing it, to make a point.

I show him a picture on my phone of Dash sitting on a pony, but when I look back at him, he's not looking at the photo. He wants me to stay; we could have another drink, he says, but I know I have to go. When I stand up he takes his own book from his bag, scribbling in it as I pull my coat on, then gives it to me. He says that he's doing an event soon, near Oxford, and he hopes I'll make it. When he leans forward to kiss me, he pulls me close to him and holds on a little longer.

In my hotel room, I look at his book. He has written in the front of it, an inscription for me: 'I could talk to you forever Clover'. I stare at his sharp biro writing, running the tip of my thumb over it, and I sense something in me that's potentially dangerous, as though poison has suddenly spilled around me. I snap the book shut. I think of Pete and home and the children, and feel I am watching them all from the other side of a motorway.

Before I go to sleep I call Pete. I want to tell him how much I love him, and I desperately want the sound of his voice in my head before I close my eyes. His phone rings out. I text him: *I love you, I love you with all my heart, I love you with all parts of me, I love you always.* Then I turn the light out and try to make my breathing quiet. When I have been lying in the dark, maybe for a few moments but maybe for an hour, my phone pings.

We've run out of milk, Jimmy texts me.

Pavel is worried about his friend, who has got pregnant in order to keep her boyfriend interested. We are in the kitchen, he is sorting laundry and I am feeding Lester.

'I'm afraid she will be all alone,' he says. 'She doesn't see the man. He isn't good. He doesn't want her to move into his flat now. What will happen when baby arrives?'

He is right. Having a baby to 'bring you closer together' is like breaking your leg in order to make running a marathon easier. Pete and I have moments of entrancement together as parents, especially when we go in to look at the children when they are sleeping and their swollen, smooth features make them look like

Raphael's most enchanting cherubs, but the feelings we also regularly share as parents are irritation, exhaustion and separation. Sometimes it's hard to remember the romance of having brought these children into the world together, although it's there, like tiny, tiny flashes of minute, pleasurable electric shocks. I used to think that parents must spend quite a bit of time staring into the Moses basket at the tiny being they'd created together. Actually the thing that's made me feel most united with Pete recently is trying to work out how to stop Jimmy playing with knives at school.

It's hard to imagine this before you embark on this trip. It's very difficult to conceive of the work involved in bringing up a child, to understand that having a baby will be like living with a little fire that needs tending all the time. Also, that being parents will change something in your relationship so that you are no longer equal. However much you want it to be something you will share, the chances are, based on all current evidence, that the mother will carry the domestic load. It won't happen straight away. Immediately after the baby is born, for the first bit, you'll feel bound together. Life and your relationship will feel exhausting and over-whelming but also cute and cosy with a new baby to snuggle. And then, a few weeks or a few months later, you'll find yourself kissing your partner goodbye as he leaves the house to work while you turn around to fold a pile of laundry and work out what's for supper.

Not me, you say. I can hear you. You don't think you will? Really?

Think hard about this. Someone has to go out to make a living when the baby is newborn. But also,

who's going to fill the fridge? Pick up the clothes
dropped on the bathroom floor to put in the washing
machine? Sit with the baby and read cardboard books
before he has his third nap of the day? Mash the banana
and rinse the bottles and turn up every afternoon at the
school gate at 3 p.m.?

I know, I know, I know. This isn't everyone. I know
there are men who do this, who are the primary carers
in their families. There is the father who is a hugely
visible presence at Evangeline's ballet class every week.
He runs up and down after his toddler daughter, speaking loudly to her about why she's a funny little monkey.
But he is surrounded by women. They are the rule, not
the exception, because this is a small provincial town in
the south of England and the majority of parenting,
Monday to Friday, from school drop-off to teatime, is
still predominantly women's work. Stand at a school
gate and look around: there are men there, but they are,
still, heavily outnumbered by women.

'I'd do almost anything in the world for another baby.
Anything. Split up, even, as long as I was pregnant. But
I wouldn't stop working,' says Kathryn to me one afternoon when we have met near her work. I have Lester
with me, so we abandon the idea of a cafe and walk
briskly around a park, him in a buggy so we can talk.
Kathryn has been having trouble with a new boss, and
she looks angry. 'I need to work. It's income, of course,
not as much as he earns, but a big part of what we live
on every month. But more than that, I need to do it.
For me. To keep hold of a part of me and who I am,
separate from the girls.' Kathryn thinks motherhood

hurts so much because we're constantly struggling to reconcile the things we want to do and the things we have to do for our children. She says her boyfriend leaves the house without ever, *ever* thinking about supper. Then she tells me about the week before, when her boyfriend called her during a week he was working away, and their daughter was ill and off school.

'And it was the week I was supposed to be managing the new intake at work. I couldn't leave early or take a day off. And he called me from his team-building week. He said he was going for a curry with some colleagues. And I hate curry. I never eat curry. But at that moment I would have done anything to be away for a week without thinking about how to work and be at home with the girls all at the same time. I would have done anything for a curry then, but instead I'd spent the week begging help from friends, negotiating with my boss to get back earlier, trying to bribe my mum to come and help me. And he was not aware of any of this. But, at the same time, I know I take it on myself. I want to be in control. I want to be the one who knows about the school play and when parents' evening is.'

We pause, leaning up against some railings in front of a pond where some ducks guddle, upside down in the water. And then she starts talking, without looking at me or making eye contact, telling me about a meeting at work, which had run on, and she'd ended up staying after hours with a man who works beside her, in a neighbouring department. She'd seen him several times, to meet up and talk about work.

'But sometimes it goes on to family life. He's married; he's got kids and so on. So nothing is happening, I know that. But he makes me feel something. Interested. *Interesting*. Alive in some way. Recognized. And definitely very separate from the rest of my life. It's funny.' She flushes. 'It's nothing really. He's only texted me. And we had lunch once. It was nice. We didn't talk about work at all then.' She turns to me, raising her eyebrows. I ask her if it makes her feel different about wanting another baby.

'By reminding me what else is out there, you mean?' she asks, pulling at a clump of her hair that's stuck to her lips. 'Maybe. A bit. Sort of. Not really. Maybe if I was a father. I wouldn't mind having a go at being a father.'

The sense of entrapment I feel is not Pete's fault, but I want to blame someone and he is the only person I can, apart from myself. I'm grateful for the work he does and the way he supports all of the children equally, but when he walks through the door after ten days in America I want him to recognize the sacrifices I've been making, the domestic chores that have replaced real thought. Being a mother at home who does freelance work in the cracks of time in between the school gate, swimming lessons and mealtimes has made me angry. And as well as making me angry, it's made me crave the full heat of his attention. I have been so angry at being left alone all day with a baby that I want to slide a knife into Pete's throat, but I've also longed for him so deeply that I crave his arms around me and his face close to mine. I want to taste him and smell him. The resentment and desire take a while to shake down, so that we can talk to one another without pecking at each other.

Later that night, after the children are in bed, he tells me about the trip. He went to stay with an old friend whom he knew as a teenager. She works for an IT company and lives in a big house in San Diego. He told me that they had sat up talking about the choices we all make, and she had said that she was finding the mix of family and work life really difficult. 'She didn't exactly say she doesn't like being a mother, but she said that motherhood was hard.'

Somehow, hearing this from another woman was deeply reassuring. I have seen her on Instagram and I have imagined that she ran her life, and that of her family, with a control and order I could never achieve. I'd visualized her leaving her tech company, where other people do what she asks, to return to her home and the big shiny kitchen overlooking the ocean. That had looked like the perfect life, I'd thought, taking my frustration out on how hard I could throw clothes into the washing machine. It was a relief to hear it wasn't, but I was surprised; if women talk about the struggle, it's usually just to one another.

'How did she say it? What did she actually say?' I ask.

'She just talked about how hard it was trying to be there for her children, and also work. I got the sense she wanted to do it all, just like you. And she also said that she didn't especially enjoy it. She said, "I don't absolutely love being a mother, like Clover does."'

'Why does she think that I absolutely love it more than she does?'

'Because you've been doing this for a long time. And you have five children. People think that you must love it, like an expert.'

I don't want to tell him that I don't love motherhood all the time. People assume that because you have
three, four, five children, you must be a natural. 'An
earth mother. You're an earth mother.' That's been said
to me so many times, but I am not an earth mother. It
does not all come naturally. And articulating the fact
that I don't love it all the time makes me sound ungrateful for what I have been given. And it sounds wrong.
Because I love my children more than anything in the
world. But loving my children is different from my
feelings about myself as a mother. The two things are
quite different.

Later I cuddle Evangeline as she lies in bed. Suddenly I
realize that she is silently crying in my arms.
    'I know I am five. I know I had a birthday party. But
most of the time, I don't feel five.'
    I smooth her hair on her pillow, snuggling my face
into the back of her neck, cradling her warm little belly
in my hand. She rolls over to face me and we talk for a
bit, whispering so Dash doesn't wake up. We talk about
growing up and birthdays, and how getting taller and
bigger doesn't always mean you're growing up.
Evangeline is one of the smallest in her class, but one of
the oldest, something that troubles her. As the first to
have reached five in her class, she feels she should be
the tallest. Her fiveness should shine out from her.
    And I realize that what Evangeline is articulating is
what I often feel about being a mother. I have five children I adore. But when I look back to the mother I
remember, who was calm and kind and loving and
always present, I don't feel like that. I feel impatient,

distracted, irritated, bored, failing, as I run around looking for lost clothes and unsigned permission slips,
swearing at baby seats that won't fit and buggies that
won't fold and teenagers who think I haven't noticed
they're telling me lies. Motherhood feels so different
from the way it looked when I was a child.

7

The Long Haul Through Every Day

Although my hunt through his room was fruitless, I know Jimmy continues to smoke weed. With his friends, anywhere but home, is where he wants to be. He wants to go up to the Ridgeway to listen to repetitive beats and get high.

I don't blame him. Not one bit. If I could choose between scraping squashed banana out of the carpet on the stairs before wrestling Dash into bed and then finding the separate pieces of Evangeline's PE kit spread around the house, or being on the Ridgeway surrounded by the night, with a racing heart and vanishing reality, I'd definitely choose the drugs.

Of course I cannot tell him this. But I'm aware that my ability to control what he does, whom he spends time with and where he goes is receding. When I find some king skins in his backpack, I dump them in the bin, but they are replaced a few weeks later and we go through the same charade again. I go through periods of trying to withhold the two sources of freedom he has: cash, and his phone. This might work for a few days, but then he needs to get a late bus back from school after a trip and I can't make plans with him without a phone. And he needs money for the bus.

My attempts to tighten the leash are haphazard and erratic. My energy for the relentless policing that being the mother of a teenager requires dissipates in the face of the needs of the younger children. I feel like the polystyrene box Dash breaks up into a thousand little pieces in the kitchen. I'm everywhere and completely ineffective.

Just before Christmas, while Lester plays with the tinsel and wrapping paper on the kitchen floor, and there is tangerine peel in the bin in the bathroom and the silver foil of mince pies littering the children's bedroom, Jimmy goes to London, to complete the work placement at the artist's studio that he missed at the end of last term. Driving him to the train station, I can almost sense him visibly breathing out at the prospect of leaving our house for a prolonged period. He stays with a friend of mine, another mother who has a teenage daughter Jimmy is friends with. I give him enough money for his tube travel across London every day and to buy lunch, and release him.

We speak on the phone every night. With distance between us, and something other than school as a subject, it's easier to talk. Jimmy is working in a studio alongside the artist and the dozen or so people who assist him, making huge metal sculptures. By the end of the week, Jimmy has started welding. The artist takes him seriously. Something in Jimmy's voice changes. There's a lightness, as if he can suddenly see the world more clearly from the outside.

I pick him up from the station just before Christmas, unable to stop myself waving at him, excited, as I see him loping down the platform, and he smiles when he catches sight of me.

No longer a place to trap him, the car journey home is a bubble where we can remember each other again before he is engulfed back into family life. There are no silences in our conversation and we talk in a joined-up way. Jimmy does not look at his phone once but speaks animatedly about what he did at the studio. It's as if he's discovering new rooms inside him that will become his adult self, and I catch a glimpse of a grown-up Jimmy whom I long to meet. Because seeing him moving out into the world, even for a few days, reminds me how much I want to catch him on the other side, when we've got through all these school days. I want to go on talking to him like this, really seeing him, without the recriminations or conflict which hang between teenage boys and their mothers.

'I definitely know now that I want to go to art school, later, after my GCSEs, after my A levels,' he says, and I'm immediately thinking of the notepads full of inventive line drawings of traps and dens and machines he's done with a biro since he was small. We have sometimes spoken about what he might do after school, and I've found it hard not to push him towards a path that's familiar to me. ('Are you *sure* you don't want to do English? I think you should do English.')

But now there is a resolve in the way he talks about a possible future which is nothing to do with me or what I visualize for him. He tells me about what it was like working as part of a team of adults. And the city. He loved walking through the city, sparkling by night, finding a new world that's far away from our life, deep in the country, surrounded by fields and so many children. It's like a sudden chink of light in the darkness of the December night, a spotlight through the thick fog of teenage life and maternal control, which reveals something about the man Jimmy might become.

We start talking about the previous few months, and the years of his early teenage life. He does not blame me but he describes something which I know is his perception of my absence from him, lost in motherhood, and his sense of losing me to all the younger ones, again and again. But he also wants to know how they are. The only time he picks up a phone is to look at pictures of his younger sisters and brothers. He shows me a tiny toy mouse he bought for Evangeline.

'She told me she really wants a mouse from Father Christmas, you see,' he says. 'I need to buy something good for Dolly and Dash, too. And Lester.' His openness almost breaks my heart, and I know that too soon we'll be back at the house where talking like this will be impossible. So I make an excuse to take the longer route home, stopping at a garage to get more milk for Lester, because I want to talk to him about the chaotic jumble that our lives have become, for the fact I haven't really *seen* him for months. I *wanted* to be more present. It's just that all the work of family life got in the way.

'It's all a lot of work,' he says, and we're quiet for a bit before, very gently, as if we're rolling a fragile bauble between us, we start talking about his schoolwork, and how smoking weed is a way of getting a release from both school and home, but that it doesn't really help.

'No, it doesn't help,' says Jimmy quickly. 'Good fun, but it doesn't help me revise.'

The familiar roads around our house rush up, and I know we only have a few moments more together.

'Let's *both* do something to make a difference,' I say, trying to temper my voice so I don't sound too zealous. And we make a bargain: he stops smoking weed until after his exams, and I'll give up the glasses of wine that litter the week when I'm jagged. As we pull up to the house, I can see the little fair heads of Dash and Evangeline bobbing up at the window, lit by the coloured light of the Christmas tree behind them. I know that they will be bursting to run out of the house and fling themselves at Jimmy. We pause for a moment, engine still running, before the swell of family life returns. Jimmy takes a big breath. He stares ahead, but he's addressing me.

'Mum, you know I missed everyone. I know I get pissed off but I missed it here. I missed the kids and Dolly. You. Pete. Everything. The noise and chaos. Pablo. I missed it all.'

The change happens, slowly. Jimmy gets off the school bus and, rather than instantly vanishing to his room, he comes to find me, at my desk or in the kitchen. Sometimes he shows me some sketches he's doing for his coursework; other times he tells me a joke he heard on the school bus, or shares a GIF he has made. Late in the evenings, when the house is finally still, we circle around each other. We talk a lot. Sometimes we watch something on Netflix together.

At parents' evening, towards the end of the spring term, a teacher tells me Jimmy is working well and has a lot of potential.

'You should feel very proud of him. A lovely young man. And he could make a fine designer, if that's the route he goes down,' he says, and I feel the yellowy pleasure of glowing relief.

The teacher is very nice. He smiles a lot and has very short black hair.

'He had that cheeky-chappie look,' I say to Pete later, in the kitchen where we are talking after the children are in bed. 'Like he probably gets stoned at the weekend.'

Jimmy wanders into the kitchen at that moment to open the fridge, laughing at what he hears.

'Are you sure teachers actually have lives?' he asks, bemused. 'You know, separate from school?'

One day after school I'm in Aldi with Dash and Evangeline, piling apples, yogurts, nappies and Ryvitas into a trolley as Lester sits in the seat in front of the handles. He clings on with amazement at his new fair-ground ride, wide-eyed at all the colour flashing past, while Dash and Evangeline hold the sides of the trolley, knocking into a pile of loo paper, screaming when we pass the biscuits, shrieking as I pause too long beside the crisps, throwing themselves on the floor with longing in front of metal bins of Paw Patrol and My Little Pony branded slippers.

But then they are suddenly quiet, embarrassed, when they glimpse a teacher from Evangeline's school filling her basket with bread rolls, Battenberg cake, eggs, a bottle of tonic water, pouches of cat food.

Evangeline pulls at my sleeve, hissing something at me so at first I think there must be some kind of desperate emergency, like the need to go to the loo or buy a chocolate bar RIGHT NOW. She tries to point while whispering to me behind her hand at the same time. Dash suddenly starts waving manically.

'Look, oooohhhh, a teacher! Evangeline's teacher! Her teacher!' he says, a crazed fan, climbing on to the edge of the shopping trolley to get a better look, as if a cartoon character has suddenly come alive in the frozen-foods aisle.

To their childish minds the idea that a teacher is a person existing outside their world in the classroom, someone who does something more than hold authority over them and chivvy them into assembly, is extraordinary, almost magical.

I am reminded of how the otherness of teachers continues into secondary school after Dolly makes a new friend whose father is actually one of *them*. 'And Rhianna told me that once she went round to their house, and lots of other teachers, you know, from school, were there. Eating Chinese take-away in, like, normal clothes. Jeans and tracksuits. Stuff like that. Rhianna said it was really weird. One of them was wearing shorts.'

And I realize that as parents, like teachers, we work hard at creating an illusion for our children of a life that is ordered, in which we are the higher authority with a clear view on how things should be. I try to create an illusion that I am in control, especially with the younger children. They need it to feel secure. But I think this changes in adolescence. The boundaries are becoming less clear and sometimes I want to show Jimmy that I'm also making this up as I go along, that like him I often want to kick back against it all. To walk away, even.

Once, when Evangeline was about a year old, Pete and I went to a party in London. We got a babysitter to stay overnight, and took the bus from Oxford, where we were living then. I'd beaten off post-natal depression and recently stopped breastfeeding, and so before I'd even reached for a single drink I had that wild, glazed look of a woman who has spent too long with her breasts exposed in the company of toddlers. I was drunk on the idea of a party before I'd even drunk anything.

It was in a basement bar, and the reward when we arrived was finding friends from university, talking over thumping loud music, and sometimes shouting at each other to explain the choices in life we'd all made. Our conversations made me think of a live version of the special visual exercises Dolly sometimes does to help her dyslexia: compare and contrast the two pictures, explaining why you prefer one over the other, or one is more successful than the other. At the party, it was compare and contrast how your career, home, weight, social life, family configuration, all shaped up alongside those of the people you met when you were on the cusp of adult life, at eighteen.

It was probably this rising pressure that made me swallow shots of frozen vodka very quickly, because I wanted the immediate focus of the evening to vanish. As long as I could see Pete across the other side of the bar, I felt safe, even if the noise and heat in the room were already making me feel slightly sick. When I looked at him, I felt completely reassured by the choices I'd made.

We both drank extremely hard that night, peeling out of the bar with the last stragglers, stopping in the street to laugh at something ridiculous, then walking further to smoke cigarettes, then banging into each other and laughing again before something in the drink made us turn on one another, and we started fighting.

I don't know now why we argued. I was so drunk I probably didn't know then, either. So drunk I could barely focus, I walked away from Pete and he turned his back on me. Afterwards, I tried to sift through the muddy water of memory to recall where I thought I was going. I know I walked into a tall town house where the people and lights of a party in full swing lit up the windows. I remember leaning up against a tall white wall and trying to talk to a man from Rome, pretending I could speak Italian, a language I know nothing of. Later, I walked down a familiar street to the bus back to Oxford, but it was early morning and I had to wait at the stop. I have an alarming, inky memory of then getting into a car with two women and a man who were all chain-smoking. I knew I needed to find Pete, and they said they'd help. When we couldn't find him, they just drove on anyway, because it seemed funny. There was a sense we were all driving around looking for something important, but the emptying streets and the music on the car radio were also amusingly distracting. And when we didn't find the thing we had all lost, they dropped me, cheerily, back at the bus stop, before driving off, tooting their horn.

I remember feeling so cold and drunk as I waited for the bus again that I was shaking, and then the man from Rome walked past, and we smoked a cigarette and spoke Italian until the bus arrived. It was, altogether, an absolute warren of rabbit holes that I'd stumbled down.

I had to persuade the bus driver to let me on as I'd lost my phone, my purse and my ticket, then I slumped in a seat as the bus sped off down the motorway to Oxford. I awoke as it pulled in to my stop, and as I stood up, Pete got up from another seat behind me. He'd caught the same bus, from an earlier stop, but we'd both been too drunk to realize.

We clung to each other in the lamplight as the bus groaned away again, as if we'd been reunited after several years of separating war. I recall feeling immensely relieved and deeply, completely happy to have found him as sobriety tightened around us and we trundled back home through Oxford, briefly acknowledging how bizarre our behaviour had been, but congratulating ourselves on our reunion.

We were parents, and we were supposed to be accountable. Responsible, even. We should not have behaved like that because parents are not supposed to be like huge toddlers, even though crashing around and making a mess is exactly what I often want to do as a parent, rather than tidy up all the time.

We crawled into bed together, shivering and giggling, and an hour later Evangeline started crying from her cot. Because we are parents, we gathered up all the control we'd shrugged off the night before and sat in the park rocking Evangeline's buggy as Jimmy and Dolly ran around us, wrestled grated cheese over some boiled pasta to call lunch, found a cartoon to distract and divert by dusk, then pretended we had the authority to get them back into bed at the end of the day.

Sometimes I think that a lot of parenthood is like that morning, trying to create an impression that you know what you are doing and are in control. Adult life is like this. The teachers have an authority and control over their class, but at the weekends, they want to relax and eat Chinese takeaway in their leisurewear. Sometimes it all feels like an illusion. The angry headmistress exercising zero tolerance really wants to get stoned too.

Perhaps this is why I find the school gate so difficult. It shows up my acting. When I should be chatting about the upcoming film club to another mum, I'm actually running my hand through Dash's hair trying to work out if he has nits. I like smiling and laughing with the valiant school secretary, but I'm not very good at making my voice sound bouncy and happy every single morning when just getting out of the door with the children in uniform and socks and shoes has made me cajole, beg, scream. Most of the time, I'm rushing through the playground, holding my children's hands and talking to them about their costumes for the school play while my mind's really gone mad with big adult worries and feeling that life might teeter out of control at any moment. After that I have to get back into the car, sometimes to sit with the radio on playing music, pretending to be looking at my phone, when really I'm just trying to piece my head back together after the rush of the morning. Sometimes the effort to make all this happen, every day, makes me cry.

When I've been crying a lot, I remind myself it's because mothering a baby makes you feel very, very tired. Lester wakes a lot in the night, and so do Dash and Evangeline. These nights are busy. Then, I try to get under the duvet early, to watch *Friends* with Dolly or David Attenborough with Evangeline. Unlike Dash, who just roars with laughter, Evangeline makes little maternal noises when she sees images of baby monkeys.

'Oh, please. A monkey. A baby monkey,' she says, tears brimming.

Eventually, I give in. I have enough monkeys so instead drive to Swindon on a Sunday evening to buy a pair of rabbits and a hutch. I'd had to chat for over thirty minutes on the phone to the lady selling them. She was moving to Singapore and wanted to make sure they were going to a good home. She sounded kind and soft, referring to the rabbits as 'bunnies' all the way through the conversation. I promised they'd be very loved and when I told her I had five children she made a funny sound like a cry and a laugh together.

'You're so brave!' Then she asked me my name.

'Clover. My name is Clover,' I said and I heard her laughing all the more.

'Clover? That's your name? Like a bunny!'

I wasn't lying when I said they'd be loved, as the bunnies spend more time in the house being stroked by Evangeline and Dolly than they do in their hutch. Or they lope around the kitchen table, twitching their noses, animated as cartoons, when Evangeline holds out slices of apple. Lester watches them from his high chair, laughing with his mouth open, the first nubs of white teeth appearing through his gums, banging his plastic spoon on his plate when they finish nibbling through a piece of lettuce.

While they are distracted by bunnies, I try and spend more time with Jimmy on his own, to continue to disentangle us both from the knots of the younger children. Most of all I want him to keep talking to me. One day he says he can't face macaroni cheese again, so I take him to a tapas restaurant so we can order the kind of food the other children won't eat: spicy peppers, anchovies, potatoes with chilli. It's like escaping, to leave Pavel to manage the mayhem, but as we settle in a window seat I feel pleased with myself: making time for my teenage son alone feels just as important as getting up in the night to comfort Lester, or listen to Evangeline practise her reading.

'Padrón peppers,' says Jimmy, interrupting my thoughts, the menus between us. I look up at him quickly. 'Did you hear me? Can we get some more peppers?'

'Yes, definitely, lovely,' I reply. After we've ordered I ask him about school.

'We always talk about my work.' He grimaces, fiddling with a salt cellar.

'OK. What do you want to talk about?' I ask brightly, before our conversation is interrupted by a waitress with our food, who makes an elaborate fuss of naming all the different plates with a strong Spanish accent. When she's gone, Jimmy surveys the food, all spread out, then looks back at me.

'Do you know you can buy a whole cooked roast chicken for two pounds? In Tesco,' he says, before pointing out that a plate of thinly sliced chorizo costs £6.80 here. We agree that two pounds for a whole chicken is good value.

'But would you want to eat a whole chicken that had been cooked at Tesco?' I'm relieved that we've found something other than schoolwork or weed to talk about.

'I wouldn't mind. I mean, two quid. Me and Dan already have, in fact. At lunch yesterday. We ate one each,' replies Jimmy. And as the words fall out of his mouth, he suddenly turns his head to the window, examining the clear glass very intently. He knows that I know that what he has just said has incriminated him.

'But you aren't allowed out at lunchtime, are you?' I say quickly. 'Jimmy? What were you doing in Tesco? Why weren't you at school?'

'Well. It was an exception, a one-off. We didn't take long anyway,' he says quickly, but we both know he's lying. He looks angry with me, as if by my finding out that's he's been skiving, I'm the one who's in the wrong. 'Look, Mum, I didn't do anything wrong. I only went out of school for twenty minutes and that was to buy a roast chicken. It was just a roast chicken.'

Actually, I want to laugh. I find the idea of Dan and Jimmy wolfing down a brace of roast chickens in Tesco car park very funny, but instead I stare at him, trying to read the truth in his eyes.

I lurch into yet another lecture, reminding him that it'll only be his future he's messing up if he starts smoking again, and that if he gets caught smoking at *school* he'll be kicked out again, except that this time it won't be a managed move, it will be an expulsion and there won't be any schools near home to go to, and if he doesn't get a proper education, he won't get a proper job and then where will he be? Just because he couldn't be bothered to go to lessons now. And he shouldn't be skiving school and he certainly shouldn't be taking drugs, right now before his exams, if he wants to get anywhere.

Jimmy stares into the distance through the glass. 'Yeah, sure, I know,' he says wearily, and he slowly spears a piece of calamari. He dips it in mayonnaise without making eye contact with me, because my words have run out. I've run out of the energy it takes to manage a teenage boy.

When Jimmy and Dolly were small children I had a friend whose seventeen-year-old son was caught stealing a car. Until then there had been a few minor misdemeanours, like being caught with cigarettes at school, an unusually high number of detentions, a general disinclination to do homework. Up to that point my friend had spent a lot of time trying to persuade her son to take his life seriously and warning him what the consequences of messing up exams can sometimes be. He ignored her and carried on, as teenagers will do.

When he stole the car, she kicked him out of the house straight away. He went to stay with a friend of a friend and told her he wasn't coming back, that he could look after himself. It was ten days before he could persuade his mother he should come home. He had to beg her to finish his education. I really admire her toughness. Her decisiveness once a certain line had been crossed cut through all the anger. And the last few months have shown me that I don't really know how to be angry with Jimmy. I hate shouting at him. I hate being in opposition to him. I hate having to tell him what to do, as if I know, and zero tolerance doesn't work. Maybe I should have been tougher, more like my friend.

'Honestly, Mum, we went out for a fucking roast chicken. A roast chicken! Two, in fact,' says Jimmy, lifting his hands up, pleading to me across the table to be reasonable, and I say to him, 'OK, OK, I get it.'

It's pitch-black when we drive home, through the startling darkness of countryside. When I complain about how dark it is, Jimmy reminds me it was my and Pete's decision to move here and that city life would have been much better.

'We should have stayed living in Oxford,' he says. And then he pauses, as we round the curve near the railway bridge that means we're close to home. And as I slow close to our gate, I'm aware of another presence, a white shadow swooping gently beside us, just beyond the glass of the window.

'Mum, an owl, a barn owl, look, Mum,' says Jimmy quickly. I slow and we look out at it, our own reflections staring back at us as the barn owl seems to turn its round face to us before it vanishes, ghostly, across the field.

'See, Jimmy, life might *seem* more fun in the city but there would be no barn owls.'

'True. No owls.' He grins at me and we both snigger a bit. 'Shame.'

Evangeline's rabbits are out in a hutch on the lawn when Alex arrives in a long dress and white trainers for tea with her daughter and baby. Lester looks up from his high chair when he sees the baby, swivelling his head around, clocking another of his kind and staring with almost indecent interest. We sit them up side by side in chairs, and they watch one another.

Much of the time Alex and I spend together with the babies involves posting food into them to stop them crying. I had bought an extra cheap Ikea high chair just for her, so that they could sit together. It's one of those white plastic ones you see in pubs. I had given up on the wooden high chair I bought at a car-boot sale one bank holiday when I was pregnant with Evangeline. It was lovely, with a faded-orange padded seat and wooden rails with coloured beads along the front of the tray that I thought my unborn baby might learn to count with. Eventually, the battle of trying to dislodge encrusted Weetabix from those wooden bars and coloured beads defeated me.

'I think that the fourteen pounds I spent on this high chair might be the most useful money I've spent on any of my children,' I said to Alex. She had just taken a cot and some bags of old toys and clothes to a charity shop, and was feeling triumphant and also a little melancholic.

'It was a relief to get rid of a lot of crap, but it made me sad too, because I won't have another baby, not now,' she says, explaining how her daughter also had a meltdown in the shop when she realized Alex was handing over some of her toys to be sold.

'My mistake. I should have done it on my own. It was insane. You'd have thought I was trying to drop her off to sell instead of her toys,' says Alex, pausing with a teaspoon of scrambled egg in front of her daughter's mouth. 'I try so hard to be calm for them, but no one warns you how your children will take you through a torrent of emotions on an almost daily basis.'

I cup my hand around the back of Lester's neck, supporting his head as I wipe yellow blotches of scrambled egg from his face. He wriggles away from me, suddenly looking furious at the warm dishcloth with tea leaves flaking from it that I've used to wipe his face with, and starts screaming at me as Alex continues talking. 'You have to do all of that and keep your head surrounded by this,' she says, gesturing vaguely at the bombed-out kitchen: a sea of garish-coloured plastic; plates of half-eaten egg littering the table; plastic spoons cast aside; a glass lying in a pool of water on the table; food, sticky and everywhere.

Upstairs, there is a crash and a screech from Alex's older daughter, who is playing dolls with Evangeline in her room. Alex jumps up as if she's been bitten, looking stricken. 'What was that? What's happened?' she says, colour sliding from her already pale face.

'It's OK, don't worry, I can hear them talking, they'll be fine,' I say, hoiking Lester on to my hip as I run upstairs. The girls have upended a book shelf and pulled a sheet across it from the bed.

'We were making a camping school,' says Evangeline, completely in control of a room that looks like a tsunami has been through it. 'It's fine, Mummy, I want it like this. Go away now.'

I reassure Alex, back downstairs.

'I worry a lot. Maybe it was from losing so many pregnancies, but I worry something bad is going to happen to the girls, a lot of the time. I want to protect them, but I also want them to be strong, maybe to compensate for my own fears. And at the same time I feel that, as a mother, I'm being babied a lot of the time. I often don't feel like I'm living an adult's life.'

She starts telling me about something that happened to her at a baby group the previous week. 'This woman said to me that the dress I was wearing, a sort of pinafore thing, was a lovely dress, when I was *mummed up*. And I had to have a long conversation with her about crafts. She wanted me to organize the next craft event. I don't understand why I am supposed to be good at craft because I'm a mother. My mother never did craft with me. She read to us and things like that, but she would never have been expected to make flowers from egg cartons. But now craft is seen as a part of parenting. Everyone seems to do it all the time. And I don't want to. I can't do it. I'm crap at it. People think I'll be good at it, but I'm crap at it.' She looks, suddenly, uncharacteristically angry. Alex never looks angry. I tell her that she always looks like she's doing a much better job at mothering than I am. She looks in control. Maybe that's why people think she's good at crafts.

'I try to remind myself to enjoy the good bits. When everything is relatively calm,' she says, wiping the spoon her daughter has dropped on a tea towel. 'And I wouldn't ever, ever go back to being not a mother. But it's lonely, isn't it? The time you spend on your own, and this sense that you have to give up something of your creative ego. I love my children, I really love them. I love the experience of being close to them. But when it comes to making wings for the school play, or being at the school gate every day, every single day at 3 p.m.! I don't enjoy that. It's such a prescribed life.'

I tell her that she does it well and that I have always felt envious of her.

'Maybe I question it less than you,' she goes on. 'But I struggle with it too, you know. Most of us do, I think. I don't know why we aren't more honest about this. Although it's not everyone. Some people really do love it all. There's a woman at the school gate, and I know she used to have a really high-powered job in IT running computer systems for an energy company. I know she loved that, but she's completely given it up and is now a full-time professional mother to her two daughters. She adores it. She really doesn't look like she misses anything at all. She's completely contented doing all . . . this.' She gestures again at the plates of food and the discarded toys, a tangle of Barbies with their legs stuck together and a mash-up of Sylvanians and Playmobil in a horrific plastic orgy. We start laughing.

'Maybe that's what you should get taught at antenatal classes,' I say. 'That rather than being something terrifying, birth might actually be the best bit.'

Later that evening, after Alex and her daughters have left, I hear the girls shouting at something outside on

the lawn. 'Catch it! Throw yourself on it! Catch it!'
Dolly screams as yet again one of Evangeline's bunnies
lopes across the lawn.

The rabbits escape repeatedly from their hutch,
throwing themselves from her arms when she cleans
them out. Lester watches, sitting on a rug outside the
house, and even Jimmy sometimes leaves his GCSE
revision to join in as Evangeline runs around the garden after the bunnies. Evangeline is fiercely competit-
ive, and most times she recaptures them. Once or twice
the rabbits have stayed out all night, only loping back in
when Evangeline reappears in the garden with carrots
early the next morning. It strikes me that the rabbits
have a much more eventful life than I do.

It is Saturday morning in late spring and Dolly is sitting
on the edge of my bed. She folds her legs neatly, her
movements so precise, so unlike the wild scramble of
the younger children's tiny limbs. There is a physical
ease to the way she moves. She has thick long hair she
likes to wear in plaits, and her skin is flawless. Sometimes
I worry that Dolly would really prefer white carpets,
white towels and a house of quiet order, rather than the
random anarchy which family life imposes on us. She
tucks her hand under her chin, crossing her legs.

As I dress we plan a summer party for her: camping in
the garden, a bonfire and a barbecue. Dolly has recently
got a smartphone, and has started occasionally posting
on Instagram, but there is a sweetness to her, as if a big
part of her is still untouched by the outside world. She
seems happy with the plan, but she is now asking to go
to a music festival too. All her friends are going.

I tell her that thirteen is too young to go to a festival on her own, and that there will be loads of time for that kind of thing when she's just a bit older. She rolls her eyes.

'It's so unfair,' she says. 'You went off and did all those things, travelling and festivals and all those things.'

I try and explain that I was older, much older, and that when I was thirteen I was still at home, but it's too late. Dolly storms off back to her room, and I go into the bathroom and brush my teeth, reaching for a pink towel beside the bath to wipe my face. There are small red and green flowers embroidered on one corner, and I press it into my cheeks, suddenly remembering the girl who gave it to me, on a train in Russia, near Rostov-on-Don. I say the name out loud, suddenly longing for the romance of it, because the memory of time there is clear and precise. The girl had thick dark hair, swept up above sharp Russian looks. I was travelling across Russia, deep into the south, and the woman had shared a carriage with me and my boyfriend. She had told me about her life, and when she went to get off the train she pulled the towel from her bag.

'I hope you'll always think of me when you use this,' she said before vanishing into the snow outside the carriage.

South Oxfordshire could hardly be further from the Russian Caucasus, but the funny thing is that I do: I think of her every time I wrap the pink towel around Lester's pale little body, or wrap my wet hair in it, or use it to wipe up the glass of water that Dash has spilled on my bedside table. I think of her regularly, this stranger whose life for a few moments intersected with mine.

Now, sitting on the edge of the bath, this innocuous little pink towel makes me want to return to that train, to be shuttling across a foreign land, miles from home, and stepping into the identity of someone completely different, with no responsibilities tying me down. Remembering Russia makes me think of my boyfriend at the time, too, his laugh, the sweaty, hard, sexy smell of him when he'd been drinking, his voice. I would love to hear his voice again. I dry myself off with the towel and try to put the thoughts of him away. I have to go and find Dolly, and make up. And there's homework to do, too.

But I think of him again later that day, when Pete and I take the children to a Syrian restaurant in Oxford. It's warm, condensation misting the windows, and I feel enclosed and safe there, happy to be with the children, laughing intently with Pete as a flash of memory hits me.

I was entirely in the moment, one of those rare moments of life with a big family when no one is screaming or needing anything, and everyone is, if not unified, definitely occupied. But there was something about the small, jewel-coloured glasses of sweet mint tea, the platter of lamb cutlets and plates of chopped herbs which reminded me of Russia. And then the metal door in the restaurant leading to the kitchen swung open, and a man stepped in, carrying a birthday cake, light streaming from small sparklers stuck into the top of it. He had big, dark eyes, and the restaurant was filled with a recording of folk music, with the sound of pipes and fiddles, which made me think of mountain music, I suppose. People were singing a fast, unfamiliar version of 'Happy Birthday' to a girl in the middle of the room. It disturbed me, the music and sparkling light, like suddenly stepping into a dream, and the Syrian man carrying the cake had the same dark looks and strong, hard features as the man I went back to so many times in Russia. It was a shock, but a good shock, in the way that plunging into a sea so cold it burns can be a deeply pleasurable experience. The memory was like a man's hand cupped around the back of my neck, pulling me away, just for a moment, from my children and Pete. And in that moment, when I had been happy, I wanted to go, away, to another world I had known, a world of danger and desire, distant from anything familiar, where I could be someone completely different. The world I had inhabited with that man had almost been tangible.

But then the music stops, the sparklers fizzle out, a child wails, and I smile back at my family, my darling darlings. Russia has completely gone as Evangeline grabs my arm, alerting me to real urgency, tears spurting from her eyes.

'Mum, Mum, Mum,' she wails. 'Mum, Dash has put salt in my Coke.'

Maybe it's because this flash of memory reminds me how often I feel penned in by domestic life, or maybe it's the pitch and severity of the way the children scream at me at bathtime, but that evening, I turn on Pete.

I hate myself for this, but I am angry. I had found out that the previous week he'd been out with some friends, and at the end of the evening he had continued drinking, in a hotel, alone with one of them, late, until they were both very drunk. She only has one child, a fact that would be irrelevant were she not younger, thinner, freer than me. It's probably because she only has one child that she can stay up late drinking with Pete, with my husband, the thought of which only makes me angrier.

He hadn't told me; I'd found out by idly reading his text messages. I know that nothing happened apart from late-night drinking, but the thought still makes me feel upset. And then angry.

'I tried to call you that night and you didn't answer. You purposefully didn't answer, I know it. Why didn't you tell me what you were doing when you were out so late?' I say, and I know my face looks horrible, scowling, but I feel so livid I don't care. He just shrugs.

'There wasn't any need to. I don't always tell you everything that's going on all the time. Do you tell me every time you have a conversation with another man?' he replies, and tips his head on one side, as if he knows my own guilty memories, of sitting in that bar with the writer who wanted to go on talking to me for ever. A thought of how distant I'd felt from the things I love best flashes across my consciousness.

I unravel in jealousy, dwelling with masochistic pleasure on the thought of Pete with someone else, the thing that makes me feel sick and furious but that is exciting, too. I am jealous of the idea of anyone having him, his attention and his warmth, or any part of his love, since it's mine. Pete has brought big love into my life, greater than anything I've felt before. And I love him back. I can't live without him. But the demands of our lives separate us all the time. When he comes home on a Friday night, I am absolutely desperate to bury myself in him and I hate that often all I have to offer him is a tangle of frayed edges with none of me left. Parenthood pushes us right away from one another. And sometimes the urge to step outside the demands, to come untethered, is strong. If I feel it, Pete must be feeling it too.

I storm out of the kitchen, and I go to our room, leaving him to handle the children, while I close the door and lie in darkness. Downstairs, I can hear peaks of excitement in the children's voices. Pete has turned the radio up, and they are probably dancing together. I can hear Lester laughing. I close my eyes and try to vanish, but there's a knock at the door. Jimmy comes into my room. 'You OK, Mum?'

'Sorry, Jimmy, I didn't mean to shout like that. I just . . . you know . . .'

'It's OK,' he replies, sitting on the edge of the bed, his hands stuffed into his jeans pockets.

'I mean, that's stupid. I did mean to shout. I was angry. Sorry. Just stressful, you know.'

'Yeah, I bet. Looks really bad being an adult some-times.' Then he stands up, wanders to the window and fiddles with the blind. 'Did you know you can get a flight from London to Bratislava for three euros?'

'How do you know?' I reply.

'Because Kyle at school bought one to go away at half-term.'

'And are you planning to join him?'

'No,' he says, fiddling with the blind. 'But if you did want to, you could.'

'Yes, I suppose you could. That's useful, Jimmy. Do you know where Bratislava is?'

'Of course I do. Sweden.'

'Can you buy me a ticket to Bratislava? Or Sweden? Anywhere really. I'd like to go to Bratislava for a bit. And I can't.'

'Oh, poor Mum,' says Jimmy, sniggering at me so that I reach behind me, throwing my pillow at him as he ducks. 'You know what?'

'No. What?'

'We could make a clone of you and then you could go away and no one would know you'd gone.' And as he leaves the room I hear his bold teenage laugh, then the metallic snap of a Zippo lighter.

Later, I creep guiltily back to the kitchen. Pete hugs me and I sink into him, deeply, deeply relieved to be in his arms.

'We just need to go and do something on our own,' Pete says. 'We just need to be away, to see each other again. It's OK.'

At bedtime, I find myself spending longer than usual cuddling the younger children, as if my attention can absolve me from the way I blunder around with the teenagers or hurt Pete. Lying beside them in bed, whispering to them as I close my eyes, is often easier, too, than reading. They want so many stories, and bedtime reading can feel like another monumental chore standing between me and sleep. My words stumble over one another, muddling together, sometimes slurring with tiredness. But I've read a book about how essential bedtime reading is to develop a child's intelligence, empathy, patience and IQ, so I press on, guilty. Dash has been sent a pile of old books by his godfather. The pages are a portal into the past through which I can peer, trying to catch a tantalizing glimpse of a life long ago. Certain books I'd forgotten in adult life, but which as a child were as familiar to me as my own hands, have surprised me. I prop Lester up on my lap and turn the pages of a burgundy-red cover containing black and white line drawings of Ferdinand the Bull. The world described in the book is distant and strange, a bullring in Seville full of matadors and picadors and ladies with flowers in their hair, but the images of this world are intensely familiar.

It was a story my mother read to us many times when we were children. Sometimes reading these old books makes hot tears fall into my lap which I cannot hide from the children. I have to ignore their little faces as they peer at me and the first cracks appear in my voice. But like looking through a keyhole, this is only a tiny glimpse of the past. I know that through the lock and behind the door is a beautiful, colourful room full of books, toys, tapestries and all the rich pictures and patterns of my childhood. I can never reopen the door, but I can push the children into the space. While they are still small enough I must help them find the way into the deepest, most colourful sense of childhood that I can dream up for them.

Later that evening, Lester turns his face away when I pull my T-shirt up to feed him. He strains and pushes his fists against me, almost crying. My body aches; my breasts don't feel flooded with milk as they had done. They feel soft, emptied of milk. I'm no longer juicy with maternity. I feel a sense of redundancy, a weakening of need. It's sad. And it's a relief.

I fold a blanket around my baby, zip him into his sleeping bag, and pat his back as he lays his head on my shoulder. I love the smell of him, the taste of the top of his ears, the softness of his hair. At a certain angle his chin and nose, his eyelashes and lips, are all so perfect I want to stop time. He is still my baby, even though he can eat real food and say real words. He'll walk, soon, too.

I decide to start giving him a bottle at night. I want this. I want the sense that my body is my own again, but at the same time, the thought that he's not my baby for much longer, and might be the last baby I'll feed, makes the backs of my eyes ache.

The next morning, while it's still dark, Lester sits up in his cot, and calls for Dolly.

8

Separation Anxiety

I am in that half-place, between light and dark, slipping in and out of different dimensions, eyes pressed shut, when I become suddenly, clearly aware of being watched. Through my eyelids, I can sense the presence of someone else. It's not sinister. If I woke up thinking an adult was watching me I'd feel completely creeped out. But this is something different. It's more like insistent comedy.

'I want to be called Yoke.'

I reach out my arm from under the warm duvet, the chill of our bedroom around me, and touch Dash's face. I feel his big head, his soft hair, the bulge of his cushion cheeks.

'Dashie, it's night-time.'

'I know. But I still want to be called Yoke.' Dash breathes against me and I hear him shifting from one foot to another. 'Or Flash.' He waits for me to catch up. I open one eye, trying to keep as much of myself in the realm of sleep as possible, because once I've woken properly it's highly likely I'll lie awake for all the hours until the last ten minutes before my alarm goes off, when I'll return heavily to sleep. Four fifty-three a.m. blinks on our bedside clock. 'I want those as my names.'

I want, more than anything, to stay in bed, but my desire for that seesaws with the fact that I know I'd prefer the rest of the house to remain sleeping. That will be impossible if I ignore Dash, because if he does not get my attention he will shout, very loudly, and then nobody will be asleep any more.

Heavily, my feet slopping in slippers, I creep down to the kitchen to make myself some tea, pulling Dash on to my lap, smelling the top of his head as he eats two crumpets, wiping strawberry jam all around his face. I try to hold the feeling of the quiet kitchen around us, the comforting smell of toasting crumpets warming the room's early-morning chill. I refill Dash's milk cup three times as he holds the plastic beaker with both hands, half his face vanishing when he gulps. Just drinking milk so that it leaves a mark of white across his top lip is for him a deeply pleasurable, completely delightful experience.

'You're totally delicious, Dash,' I say, stroking his cheek, and he looks at me sideways, as if he is sizing me up, suddenly serious.

'But you've never tasted me, Mum,' he says, screwing up his eyes as if he doesn't understand, before reaching for the cereal box on the table. 'Weetabix now.' That's what's really delicious in his mind. I run my hand through his bright blond hair, wishing it could always be this easy.

The emerging garden outside is fuzzy with mist, pink fingers of light caressing the last film of dawn with the promise of warmth and sunshine that will follow later in the day. I pull a coat over my nightclothes and push Dash's square little feet into blue plastic boots decorated with diggers.

'We'll go outside in our pyjamas, OK, Flash?' I say, and he beams. The grass outside the house is dotted with coloured plastic toys – oversized Lego, some train tracks, a plastic play house for Evangeline's dolls – but I don't want to keep Dash in the garden, because even if he's completely quiet, somehow the rest of the children will sense we're here, and wake up.

Beyond the gate, the road curves round out of sight and the fields with the concrete path across them belong only to me and Dash. He squeezes my hand, pointing out the bush near the gate where there will be blackberries later in the year, and runs ahead to the old bright-red disused phone box. He presses his face against the panes of glass to stare inside, as though there might be a huge surprise there.

There's a green smell of late spring, and the sound of birds filling the air around us. We make good ground, just Dash and me, and I'm surprised, since when I walk with all three of them, with Lester in the buggy, one hundred yards can feel like a half-marathon of tumbling, screaming, cajoling to keep them going. Unencumbered, we walk on to a field of tall bulrushes, disturbing some ducks who fly up in front of us, making Dash shriek and jump up and down in his little boots. When he tires, I pull him up into a piggyback to keep up the momentum. When we're far from the house, we sing songs, and I make up new words to the tune of 'Scotland the Brave', about a boy called Dash who loves trains more than sweets or anything else in the whole wide world. I pull him around and into my arms, and he throws his head back as I sing to him more, wrinkling his nose up. It is delightful, but I'm also so tired I want to lie down in the damp rushes to sleep.

'Shall we go back home now, Flash, and have some more milk?' I suggest, but his face darkens and rather than laughing, he opens his mouth to scream, a banshee wail that echoes through the trees around the field. It's the noise he'd make if I stabbed him, or if he was summoning the energy to stab me. Suddenly his eyes aren't bright and smiling, but wet with tears. 'Dash. OK. We'll walk further,' I say, and he starts laughing giddily, so that he's laughing and crying at the same time. I pull him closer into my arms, and to distract him from screaming, ask him what he dreams about at night.

'Parties. I dream of all kinds of parties,' he replies.

We walk on through the long grass, Dash holding on around my neck as though I am his sweetheart. My body and arms ache, and it's not yet 6 a.m., but every time I try to exert my own will against Dash's – to go home, make a cup of tea and crawl back into bed – he starts to scream and cry again. It's better to give up or, at least, give over to him for the moment. If I forget myself and what I want, being with my small son, who cannot yet make a long walk around a field, is pure gold. I am a horse, stepping into its driving harness, shaking its head because it wants to resist for a moment before it leans forward into the collar to pull.

Later, the kitchen is full of children. Jimmy has been revising, but is taking a break by having some friends over. Sometimes I'll be persuaded to pick them up, but at other times, Jimmy and his mates walk across fields to meet one another, as if they're in a Thomas Hardy novel.

I like it when the kitchen is filled with his friends, tall teenage boys with messy hair wearing tracksuits trooping in and out, bringing a new kind of energy to the house. It's the energy of anticipation, as though they're all pet tigers about to be let out of their cages into the wild.

They go out to the lake near the house, to mess around with a yellow inflatable plastic dinghy, and return, hours later, laughing noisily when Dash and Evangeline run up to them, throwing themselves at them at the excitement of these young giants arriving in their mini-world. Dash and Evangeline want to show the boys what they have been learning all afternoon, with a box of matches and some tea-lights. Dash has learned how to strike a match into life, working his way through a big box until there's nothing left apart from a pile of little black sticks and some red marks on the end of Dash's thumb. I had taken the matches away from them to start with, but Dash had climbed on to a shelf to get them down again. Eventually, I'd let them sit on the lawn with the matches, so that they could learn, even if it meant they burned their fingers. Now they want to show the teenage boys what matches can do, and the teenagers fold their long limbs together to kneel down to their height, humouring them, before introducing the thrill of coloured plastic lighters. I am not worried. Teenagers and children: they are all looking out for one another.

Dolly has also been busy with Evangeline, cleaning out the rabbit hutch. The rabbits have, for the moment, given up their escapologist tricks and seem settled in the cage outside the kitchen window.

I am sitting on the kitchen table, talking to Pete who is back from London, when suddenly there is a scream from the garden. It's not the kind of scream the younger children make, which cuts through the day many times an hour, but the sharp, pitched scream of Dolly.

The rabbits' cage is open, and Dolly is standing in horror, because inside there is something moving. It is a nest of small, squirming, hairless rabbits, burrowing between one another, eyes pressed shut.

The teenage boys find this both outrageously funny and totally gross. They peer into the bottom of the cage, where the little naked rabbits wriggle.

'They look a bit like massive maggots,' says Jimmy.

Grim, his friends agree, laughing simultaneously, then they slope back upstairs to Jimmy's room, where they'll shut themselves in for the rest of the day. I'll still be able to hear them laughing in the furthest room.

The younger children scream and holler, running around and around the garden, celebrating the new bunnies like little coloured fans fluttering in the spring morning. Lester watches from my lap, looking out into the garden, but straining forward, pulling himself up to watch them on the edge of the sofa, because now he wants to run with them, too.

The baby days don't suddenly end. They recede slowly until you turn around and realize, one afternoon, as you catch the outline of your child's head, that the pudgy baby with the big gummy grin who bounces on your lap, gnawing at your knuckles with a mouthful of drool, the back of whose neck smells like heaven, who wants you, you, all the time, has gone.

He's gone because he's changed into a stronger version of himself as you separate. And although you feel a little less tired, and occasionally your body feels a little more springy since you've stopped breastfeeding, you also cannot deny the fact that this hurts.

Almost one year old, Lester can easily pull himself up against the pink sofa in the kitchen, unsteadily propping himself up to bang a wooden brick against the edge of the table leg. He likes to hold a collection of clattery plastic objects in his hands – the connection of a hosepipe, a magic wand and a golf ball – as if they make him feel more secure. He sleeps with a toothbrush clasped between his little fingers every night, and he likes to point his finger when he's carried across the kitchen. Silver foil entrances him.

He loves Dolly, lunging at her from my arms when she walks past. She stops and kisses his small cheeks so that he shrieks with pleasure, and then they're entangled around one another as I step back, watching from the other side of the kitchen. There are moments in each day when sibling rivalry flashes between the children. Sometimes, Dash and Evangeline will emerge from a fight over a broken mobile phone with clumps of one another's hair laced through their fingers. Dash has bitten Evangeline so hard he has drawn blood. Jimmy and Dolly will sometimes wrestle like full-grown adults when they fight, but no one will defend her as fervently as Jimmy will, when it's needed. The rivalry is there, but the love between them is much stronger.

'Come on, Lester, you can do it, you can do it,' Evangeline and Dash squeak, their little voices a chiming chorus of encouragement the first time Lester walks across the kitchen, taking three or four new, tentative steps. He pushes a stuffed-horse walker on wheels across the kitchen, its momentum propelling him along, away from me, towards them, as they wait for him with outstretched arms.

Evangeline and Dash start to involve Lester in their long, elaborate games, which always involve pulling all the cushions off the sofa and then stretching blankets between it and the kitchen table to crawl under. The world they inhabit is huge and colourful, a complex universe that I'm only ever on the outskirts of. They play parents a lot, each carrying armfuls of plastic dolls.

Sometimes I hear Dash calling, 'Mum, Mum,' and when I say, 'What is it, my darling?' he replies, 'No, not you,' because it's Evangeline he wants.

When Lester joins the gang and they rename him Borgjetta — I have no idea where they got this name from — and when I ask if he's their son, assuming he's part of their new parental camp, Evangeline looks surprised, correcting me that he's not their son but a friend. They dress him up in a peaked cap and he follows them out into the summer light.

'He wants a pet! He wants a pet of his own, I think!' squeals Evangeline as she sees him crawling towards the rabbit hutch. Soon he's walking so well he can toddle over to the hutch on his own, which turns into something of an obsession. The cold morning dew doesn't stop him, his small pink feet sticking out of dungarees in the wet grass. I often find him there, staring at the small creatures in the cage. It's as though he realizes he's no longer the smallest in the family.

The timer that my pregnancy switched on before Lester's birth is still ticking away, but the sound is less insistent. I don't count the days or weeks of his life any more, because he's almost one. Soon I'll be counting the time in years.

The house is still complete chaos almost all the time. Oranges bob around in the bath, piles of plastic toys litter the floor in every room, dolls lie face down under the kitchen table and whole shelves of books are pulled on to the floor. For some as yet unexplained reason, there are tennis racquets in every room, and not one single shoe in the hall has a pair. At least once a day I will fish a new loo roll out of the loo, and after Dash and Evangeline have been playing upstairs I find a tideline of scribbles and spidery writing on the wall saying 'ILOVE yOu' and 'LoVe from MUmMy', as if they think that will absolve them. Pens without lids are everywhere, biscuits religiously ground into the coloured rug in the playroom, sweet wrappers pushed down the back of the sofa, apple cores beside children's beds and pieces of toast nestling in the sofa. Pavel screams when he lifts up a cushion from the sofa to reveal a dead mouse.

I try extremely hard to disengage from caring about the mess a family of seven creates, reminding myself that of course no child minds or even notices. I put pots of hyacinths in the kitchen windows by the sink to distract myself from the washing-up, and hang yet more pictures over the smudges on the walls. Sometimes I find feet marks running up the edges of walls: the children take over every nook and crevice of our home.

Pavel has abandoned his attempts to organize the house which took up much of his time when he first arrived, looking appalled as he tidied shoes into pairs and muttering that the house was like a hostel. Now he just cheerily dumps boots and trainers into a great pile near the front door, just like everyone else.

Resistance to the mess mostly feels futile. An entire weekend can pass in which I feel I have achieved nothing other than carrying piles of clothes from one room to another, as they make their long, circular journey from dirty, on bedroom floor, downstairs to the washing machine and back up again, folded, never ironed but clean.

'What would your superpower be, Mummy?' Evangeline trills at me, skipping as she walks beside me while I gather up waste-paper baskets full of nappies, cups of cold tea and glasses of stale water from bedrooms.

'The male ability not to see mess,' I reply, pausing at the top of the stairs to kick a stray piece of train track aside. When she looks confused, I laugh. 'I mean, fly. I'd like the ability to fly.'

★

Kathryn visits just before Lester turns one. She looks different. Less ruffled and taut, she's smiling more.

'We've had therapy,' she says. 'Couples therapy. Because of the fighting. It wasn't good for family life, and we were all unhappy. And it was often me doing the fighting. He didn't want to talk about anything, as if by ignoring the fact that a part of me is mourning something he could make it go away. I was mourning the end of baby-hood, I suppose, the fact I won't have more kids.' She says this strange sense of sadness had defined much of her life for the previous couple of years. 'The pain was there all the time, which made me feel somehow ungrateful for what I do have. Which is huge. And I *am* grateful for that.' She says it's still painful, but that therapy has helped her look forward to the next part of life, with the freedom it might bring. 'It's not perfect, but I think I'm coming to terms with it. Although I think I'll also always hurt a bit about it.'

I ask her about the other man whom she had seen.

'Oh, nothing really happened, as in "happened". There were lots of text messages. Flirting really. Nothing physical. But he helped me to *see* myself. He allowed me to see myself as someone, you know, almost desir-able, after that feeling of being invisible, unheard, that can happen in a long-term relationship.' She pauses. 'That was all I needed. I was lost. We were lost.'

I ask if her boyfriend ever found out.

'No. But then I think he might not even notice if I was having a full-blown affair with someone right under his nose. I think we're finding ourselves again, a bit, now, though. He's a grumpy bugger, always will be, but it's OK.'

She tells me about the holiday they're planning, driving through France and into Spain and Portugal, for three weeks over the summer in a camper van.

'It sounds perfect, a proper family adventure,' I say and feel envious. 'The thought of a big, roaming holiday like that seems a long, long way away for me.'

Kathryn laughs. We both know that this kind of holiday is something she can do now her daughter is no longer a baby, or even a toddler. 'Gains. There are gains to them growing up. But you should go away, though,' she says. 'Remember who you both are. Just you two. The kids will be fine. Lester is almost old enough. You should do something on your own.'

She's right. Pete and I are in danger of seeing one another only as caregivers, of failing to even see one another at all. We need to go away before we both vanish from one another's sight.

Pavel is confident about coping with the kids on his own but I also ask a younger friend to stay, to make our trip, which will last two whole nights, more of an adventure for the children. Rachel is twenty-seven and enjoys making dens and doll's houses from cardboard boxes, and teaching Evangeline how to sew. She is fun, leaping around the kitchen in leggings and crop tops, resolutely bra-less, while Pavel cooks pasta, which he seems to do more or less continuously.

Driving to the airport past verges studded with dusty ragwort, I realize that the drama of this moment, which I've longed for and fantasized about for such a long time, feels suddenly almost overwhelming. I'm anxious without the children with me. The possibility

of an impending disaster stretches out along the geo-
graphical line between myself in Seville and the children back at home. We pass a building site close to
Heathrow, and the outline of a large package hanging
from a crane looks suddenly sinister. I try to put black
thoughts of what might go wrong away from me, texting Pavel: *Has Lester stopped crying now? Has Evangeline
eaten? Is Dolly happy? Is Jimmy still in the house? Is he
revising?*

All is fine. Don't worry. We are making pasta, he replies.

At a distance from the children, it's easy to see how
they blur the edges. I'll use a broken biro to stir a cup
of tea, or take a dishcloth straight out from the sink
without rinsing it to mop a baby's face. I'll wipe their
snot on my jeans or skip brushing my teeth because the
noise of the taps might wake Lester.

Now, alone with Pete, adult life quietly settles around
me, and it's crisp and clear and mostly within my control. At the airport, carrying my one, smug little piece
of hand luggage, I see the look of gentle despair cross
the face of a woman as she wakes her sleeping baby,
who starts crying, in order to fold the buggy to pass
through security. She calls to her husband to take the
nappy bag hooked over the buggy but he's wrestling
with their son, holding his tiny wrists as he strains and
screams to run back out towards the entrance. The child
kicks him and the man's face creases; there's a smear of
something down the front of the Oasis T-shirt he's
worn for the holiday. I feel I ought to ask the woman if
she wants help, but I can't, really, stop and offer every
woman I see in this airport with a screaming child a
hand.

Without the need to organize and herd children, the airport itself is a pure pleasure dome, rather than an assault course to be navigated without losing one of them, while simultaneously dropping forty-eight pounds on comics with plastic toys taped to the front of them, or packets of crayons that will be flung under a cafe table, or endless bottles of bright-orange smoothie, the thing all my children crave most. Instead I linger at the Chanel counter, stroking the heavy glass scent bottles filled with green liquid, as a man in a black suit swoops down beside me, handing me little white tickets to spray the scent on to. I make a play of doing this carefully with two or three perfumes, then grab a lot of bottles, layering the scents over me like expensive coloured scarves, bringing the adult world sharply into focus as I think of the woman still struggling with her buggy.

We sit for twenty minutes in a cafe, waiting for our gate to be called; just being alone with Pete, drinking coffee and doing nothing else, is a deep and complete pleasure. We laugh at each other's jokes, speak in whole sentences and both start and finish a conversation. I want to touch his face, to reacquaint myself with all of him again. More than anything I want to remember how it feels to love him, and to really see him. Absolved from being a mother, I am someone different: less harassed and calmer.

Still, on the flight, my eyes are magnetically drawn to a baby on his mother's lap across the aisle. I have to resist the urge to reach across and stroke the sweet tender nape of his neck. I have one like that, my son, but he's almost one now, I want to say to the mother, but instead hide behind the in-flight magazine, wondering whether if I buy a fluorescent plastic watch or pair of sunglasses with diamante detail, our short holiday will feel more holidayish.

When I was in my twenties, I lived on a ranch in Texas and knew a cowboy called Powder who was deeply loved by his wife, Janey. They had small children, but whenever I passed them on the dirt track that led to their cabin, Janey would be sitting right next to Powder on the bench seat in the front of his pickup. When I remarked on this to one of the cowboys, he nodded and laughed.

'Even with all those kids, Janey sure does like to sit real close up beside Powder.' I wanted to be like Janey, to meet a cowboy whom I wanted to sit right close up to in the seat.

It's how I feel about Pete, when I have time to think about him. The children squirm between us on the sofa, talk over our conversation at the kitchen table and elbow us away from one another in bed. Days will pass when we barely converse beyond making plans for the children, making plans for tomorrow. Weeks can pass when we barely touch, even when we are in bed, because there's almost always a child between us. Often, the closest we come to touching is our fingertips brushing in sleep.

Sometimes there are days when I think that cuddling Evangeline as she falls asleep, or snuggling up to Lester and Dash as I read to them in bed in their pyjamas, their limbs tangled around mine, is all I need. There are times when my skin is pressed up against that of my children, and we're breathing the same air, all hot and utterly close like we're still one person, when I feel that I love cuddling my young children more than I love sex.

But now, being alone in a hotel room with Pete, I feel an almost hysterical lightness inside me. There is an acute novelty of not being needed for caring, and instead doing something purely, absolutely for pleasure. There's the novelty of reaching across the empty space between us, and realizing that the person we find there is still the one we love the most. And the novelty of sex in the afternoon and sex in the morning because no one else is in bed with us.

Alone together we can remember what it's like to behave as people who love one another, rather than as people who have vaguely started walking through life together but are continuously separated by a herd of others. When it is just us I become someone different. I become the person motherhood separates me from. It's like waking up. It's exciting, and consoling too, this feeling that we are both still there for one another. That we have not lost each other. That we have not lost us, or our marriage.

I write a note to myself, because it's easy to forget these things: 'When motherhood is drowning you, Pete is your life raft. Do not attempt to smash him to pieces because you're angry. Cling to him. Be his life raft through these stormy waters, too.'

When we're near home on our way back I sense the wedge of parenthood nudging back between us once again. It's Sunday night so there's nothing languorous about our return from the Spanish sun. After the drama of our return, after the children have thrown themselves at us, ripped open the bags of sweets, the grit of normality returns too fast. Supper needs to be made. Bins must be put out. Too quickly I start bossing everyone about, organizing book bags, hunting for the lost lids of water bottles and a PE kit that was supposed to be washed. But I remind myself of what we have, and that night I cling to him, the life raft that's keeping me from drowning.

One afternoon in a cafe where I've escaped the house for a bit to write, I find myself observing a group of new mothers, and I realize at that moment, very clearly, that I'm no longer the mother of a baby.

What strikes me most about the mothers is their kindness, and also their humanity. They're absolutely attentive to their babies. There are conversations to be had, about the labour, about when their parents-in-law will leave or when maternity leave will be over, or whether it's time to wean, but not until they have fished the plastic pot of pureed carrot out of the bottom of the buggy, or played peek-a-boo to placate the crying, or unrolled a changing mat and found wipes and a nappy and all the endless bits and pieces that babies need.

The babies are oblivious to this labour around them, sitting in a line of high chairs, swinging their legs, staring insistently at one another, occasionally letting out a shriek of recognition. It has taken a great deal of exertion for these mothers to meet, for a short while, in this cafe, and none of them finish any of the conversations they start before their babies interrupt them with their cries, or small hands grab their hair. They are babies, though, distinct from the toddler Lester is becoming.

He won't sit up in a high chair any more, but wants to clamber across the table to crouch under it on the other side. Now that he can walk, or at least toddle a few steps before stumbling over, he is distinctly separate from me. Both Lester and Jimmy are walking away now.

Later, putting Lester to bed late on a summer evening, he reaches his hands out to the window where the white dusk sunshine seeps under his curtains. He stretches out, feeling its warmth as it glazes over his pale skin. I try to lay him down in his cot but he bounces up, jack-in-a-box, and starts crying, straining his arms towards me. I pick him up and he puts his head on my shoulder, patting my back. Sleep is a long way off. Dash is in his pyjamas, making a train track down the landing, but I grab his hand and we head downstairs, Lester on my hip, Dolly and Evangeline leaving their YouTube make-up tutorial to follow us. In the kitchen, Jimmy is slowly eating a huge bowl of Shreddies.

'Come on, have a break from revision, let's all go out for a walk, before it gets dark,' I say quickly, so that Jimmy doesn't have time to resist, because Dolly has already found shoes for Evangeline and is out of the door, Evangeline's hand in hers, calling for Pablo.

Together we walk to the edge of the lake near the house; Jimmy holds Dash's hand as I carry Lester, and Evangeline runs ahead with Dolly. There is a special sort of pleasure in walking through the long grass in the evening light, Dash and Evangeline electric with the excitement of being outside in their nightclothes.

'I like swinging through the long green grass,' says Dash, reaching up to Jimmy, who looks so huge, towering over him, then leans forward to pick him up under his armpits and swing him along in front of me as he shrieks with excitement.

We pause at the lake, the moon's early reflection simpering on its flat surface. Jimmy tells them all a story about a flying skeleton, and geese arrive on the lake, making a strange, distant, crying sound. Dash is so small, his round pale face shining up at us like a little moon. Dolly has picked up Evangeline and is soothing her, because Jimmy's tall stories scare her. Dash wants more, though. There is an edge in his voice, because he loves the stories Jimmy tells him, even though he is a bit frightened by them too. Like me, Dash wants to feel the darkness around him and to feel his heart racing faster.

I watch them silently as we walk on through the long grass, resolving to spend as much time as I can with all of them, but especially with Jimmy, before he's left school and gone. I am always trying to hold on to him. He has his A levels to do but still, I'm terrified of him going. He takes a part of me with him as he grows up. Part of the person I was as a younger mother to him leaves with him as his adult self emerges. And when I ran my hands under his pillow in his room, I was looking for clues as to who he was, but I was also looking for clues as to who I might become, later, when he's gone.

The moonlight is white on the lake, and in a flash I remember my own mother, taking my sister and me out to the field behind our house when the moon was huge and full, so that we could feel its glacial white light. I'm alone with my children but something of her is there; with the night around me and the moon shining on all five of their faces, I am suddenly, brilliantly happier than I have been since I first held Lester in my arms. I'm happier than I've been for eleven months, since I was closest to labour.

9

Every Precious Moment

Pressing her small hot body against me under the covers, Evangeline puts her palm on my face, staring at me with a look of complete and uncomplicated love. It's past midnight, but her footsteps down the corridor to our room have woken me, before she scrambled into bed in one swift, well-practised movement.

I love the smell of her body, and as I move back towards sleep, I think that in this moment I feel as close to heaven as I'll ever be on this earth. It is a seminal sort of love. Evangeline sighs deeply, pressing her back against me as she turns over, hooking my arm around her so that I'm holding her really tight.

'Do I belong to you?' she whispers, suddenly awake in the dark bedroom.

'Yes, I think so,' I murmur back at her, trying to remain asleep. 'At least, for this moment. For tonight.

And for now. But one day you won't. You'll grow up, like Jimmy. Snuggle down, let's sleep.'

Later, around 3 or 4 a.m., more children pile in. Sharp heels and elbows jab at me, pushing me to the outer edges of the mattress and pulling the duvet tight over towards them.

Fighting for the edge of a pillow is not relaxing and it's not heaven, and from 4.50 a.m. I lie tense in the dark, trying to convince my ticking brain that I can actually continue to sleep as sleeping human-size fidget spinners rotate around me. I should be firmer, and operate a one-in, one-out door policy, like a nightclub that has become dangerously full. But as dawn arrives, I'm aware of a physical change in the environment around me, a curious, uncomfortable warmth I can't identify. I lie very still, hoping it will go away. Evangeline sits up, rubbing her eyes and pulling the final little corner of the duvet off me.

'Also, now we have some pets, could we have another baby, too?' she says, as though we're in the middle of a conversation.

The warmth, I realize, has come from Dash, face down, eyes tight in sleep, as he pees in the sheets around me, a drunk in the nightclub of our bed.

I can't sleep any longer, and anyway soon an alarm is sounding, and there are lunch boxes to be jumbled together, cereal and milk to be sloshed into bowls, many teeth that need brushing.

Walking through the day I am hugged by a heavy, thick, inescapable fog of tiredness. Lester goes to a baby group with Pavel, and Dash does half a day of pre-school. I sit at my computer for a few hours and write, but I feel absent and rather unsure of what I'm doing much of the time, deleting most of my sentences soon after writing them.

But by 3 p.m. it's sunny, and high summer, so Dash, Lester and I scoop Dolly and Evangeline up from school and we go to a splash park in a small town nearby. They scramble out of school clothes and into swimmers in the back of the car, spilling out as we arrive, darting away from me and in and out of the jets of water that spurt up from the ground. Dash's beam fills the park as he runs through the splashes, hair plastered to his face. Dolly swings Evangeline around on a colourful metal roundabout, wet bodies shining in the summer afternoon. I spread a towel under the shade of a tree, stretching out as Lester toddles around after them, trying to keep up.

For a few moments I'm able to lie flat on the blanket and close my eyes, because Dolly is with them. It's so warm, and the patter of the water jets is soothing. My eyes loll, and I'm desperate to slip back to the place I was woken from so early this morning. Surely I could just shut my eyes and all would be well? I close them, the sound of summer in the park delightful around me, until I realize my children's voices have moved away, and I can't hear them. I panic suddenly, eyes snapping open, sitting up and swearing at myself as I call Lester's name. He's heading towards the water jets, but turns around when he hears my voice, falling, then crawling and walking again back towards me, patting my face with gritty hands.

When an ice-cream van arrives, the children clamour around me as we scrape together some change from the bottom of my bag, which isn't enough for four ice creams, until Dolly runs barefoot back to the car beside the park, hobbling across the gravel to locate coins discarded on the floor or in the seat pockets.

'A Feast, a Cornetto, a Solero, a Rocket, NOT Mini Milk!' Their demands surround me, voices chiming into one, jumping up to make their point like wet shiny seals, round-eyed and begging for attention. The ice creams silence them, melting orange ice dripping off Dash's round chin; Lester looks serious and slightly concerned as he eats chocolate ice cream for only the second time in his life.

At this moment, right now, leaning back on the grass, the children spread around me, Dolly slouched forward, long and slim, Evangeline lying on her tummy kicking her legs, I'm as happy as it's possible to be. It's one of the moments when being a mother is suddenly still and complete, when no one is fighting or crying or need-ing me to do anything for them, except dispose of a sticky lolly stick, or run a towel across their hair. I watch the four of them, feeling prouder and luckier than I deserve to be. These children are my vision of perpet-ual love, and I can feel a physical tug as my heart contracts.

There is a gap, though, where Jimmy should be. He's stayed at home, revising for the last of his exams. I'm always missing him. Five children overwhelm me a lot of the time, but what I crave is all of them together, the feeling of completeness, the full pack, the perfect five.

Afterwards I pack the blanket and towels and wet swimwear together, and we walk slowly back to the car, Dolly and I holding Lester's little palms between us.

Lester can only just walk, but one day, none of them will be with me. The parasol is hooked over my shoulder, and its shadow makes it look like a gun. I feel I need it to guard me against the losses motherhood will bring.

'What does motherhood really feel like?' asks Pete, later that evening, while I'm making a bottle for Lester, ready for his midnight waking, and Dash and Evangeline are thundering around upstairs in their pyjamas, but not yet in bed.

Pete is looking through photographs I'd found and left in a box on the table. In one Jimmy was about four, at a nativity play. He is wearing a cardboard crown I made for him using silver foil with wine gums stuck on to it. This is my greatest achievement in craft, ever. In the photograph Jimmy's chin is tipped upwards, as if he's proud but also a bit shy or maybe nervous, and the cloak he's wearing – an old blanket – is coming undone. I'm sitting on the floor, in some sort of community centre, surrounded by children and other mothers. We're holding children, or have children leaning on us. Dolly is in my arms, small face questioning the camera. My hair is pulled back into a ponytail, and although I was only twenty-seven, motherhood does look like it's exhausting me. There's another picture, of Dolly sitting up on my lap, aged about one, her tiny face a small round dot, as Jimmy sits beside me. He's mostly a blur in the picture, scribbling on a piece of paper, feeling fast. Pete passes me the picture and I try to remember what it felt like. Holding a physical photograph is strange; all my photographic memories of motherhood are contained within my phone. Maybe that's why I carry it absolutely everywhere and why I touch it so much. It disconcerts me when the children turn to that iPhoto function called On This Day. I like being able to see exactly what was happening on 23 May 2014 or 18 September 2017, but as I watch the smiling faces floating past, the trip to the river, the noisy teatime, the bedtime kiss, all recorded on the phone, I'm often not completely sure that I was actually there. If I am in a photograph, I'm almost always looking down, away from the camera, rarely making eye contact, often slightly absent, as if my balance is slightly off, and I'm searching for something out of shot.

'What does it really feel like?' Pete repeats. 'Motherhood, I mean.'

This is the question I've been trying to answer since I started writing about my family: what is it like, this role, which started, for me, in 1999 when I was first pregnant with Jimmy, defining the colour of most of the best and hardest moments of my life until now, and which stretches out before me like a long, long road for many more years? What does being a mother really feel like?

It's lots of feelings every day. It turns you into an eclipse, light and dark covering each other at the same time. It's like being in a trance, sleepy and absent but also deeply content. It's also like being completely present, running very quickly down a steep hill but with no time to catch your breath, your legs moving more swiftly than your body can register, the momentum propelling you forward through tasks which never seem to end until the baby becomes a toddler and then a child and then a teenager and suddenly the hill is no longer so steep and the flat ground is arriving and you're jogging, then walking. Often motherhood makes you feel you're racing so fast, there's no time to really appreciate your surroundings.

I don't have time to answer Pete, because upstairs there's a crash and the sound of running water. The children have been balancing a plastic bucket of water on top of a pile of books stacked up like a tower of cards on top of the chest of drawers beside Dash's bed.

'We were just trying to make a shower for our cats!' protests Evangeline, her pyjamas soaked to her shivering body.

'But why? For God's sake! There's water everywhere! Didn't you think it would fall?' I shout, snatching up the books to try and save them from the wet, wiping them off on the edge of Dash's duvet.

'The cats we adopted! We've been making cat carriers for them from cardboard boxes but they needed a wash,' she replies, as if it's obvious. The commotion has woken Lester, who starts screaming in his cot in his little room next door.

'But not real cats! Imaginary cats!' shouts Dash, bouncing on the bed, not oblivious to the commotion he and Evangeline have created, but excited by it.

'Also, Mum, Mum, Mum, do you know . . .?' says Evangeline, jumping up and down beside me as I strip sodden sheets from the bed. 'Leopards are actually more scared than we are when we see them in the wild. Did you know? So if we saw one outside now it would actually be really scared of us.'

'Mum, I really, really need help with my chemistry homework. I don't understand it and it's due tomorrow and I'm going to get a detention,' wails Dolly, suddenly appearing at the children's bedroom door as Jimmy storms down the corridor, shouting at us all.

'Why is it always, always so fucking noisy in this house?'

Afterwards, I put the books to dry in the airing cupboard and take Lester a new bottle to soothe him back to sleep, while Pete sits quietly with Dolly and her chemistry equations, which are way beyond my abilities. He says he'll put the kids to bed.

'Go out. Go for a walk. Go and get some space,' he says.

I leave the house, driving too fast on the bend, disturbing a handful of black crows in a tree. They gather quickly in the air in one swift movement, as if they've been thrown there, and I feel a release in my soul, like relief, in the shape they make. The losses of motherhood make my eyes fill with tears. The me that was lost. I drive on, up to the Ridgeway, and park where I shouldn't, not in the National Trust car park but on the edge of the track beyond it. I want to bust out of my containment and parking where I'm not allowed to is the feeble mark of my rebellion. I think of the question Pete asked me, and as I walk I pull my phone from my pocket and text Kathryn: *What does motherhood feel like?*

I jog on, like I'm half running away from the car and the three baby seats strapped into the back, sweet packets ripped open on the floor, crisps ground into the footwells, a naked doll and one small red wellington in the boot. I'm running into the sky now, which pulls me upwards, the light entering my head and settling there rather than splintering into something else.

Within moments my phone pings: *Guilt love grief rage despair chaos peace.*

Then a few moments later she messages again: *Drowning trapped overwhelm and abundant joy.*

I want to punch my way out of this feeling of being squashed so I walk on and on, into the huge landscape around me and the sky that holds me in it without asking me or telling me anything. It wants nothing of me. At the corner where I can turn left to walk up behind the Ridgeway, or right to Wayland's Smithy, three boys on bikes are suddenly behind me, their voices elevating into the afternoon air. I turn around and watch them, and they are completely oblivious to me.

'Come on, mate, it's this way to Wayland's Smithy,' one shouts. He has spiky black hair, a spattering of freckles across his face; he's lounging sideways as he waits on his BMX for the other two boys to catch up behind him. He leans down, balancing his bike with one hand, staring into the ground as though it's a mirror. Then he spits into the dust, watching the glob of phlegm settle at his feet before he looks up quickly, catches my eye, and like a startled animal presses his foot to the pedal and then it's his back view I can see. His two friends zig and zag past on their bikes, their voices rising and laughing, vanishing into the evening.

Along the track to the west, a field of wheat and a bolt of blue sky above it look like a child's picture drawn with wax crayons turned on their sides so that colour is made by the whole edge of the crayon, rather than the point. There's the blue and yellow, and along-side that the sticky brown of a ploughed field. The wheat shimmers, moving in one continuous ripple as the sheets do when Evangeline lies on the bed and asks me to whoosh the cotton above her head. My skin itches with the tiredness of lifting and carrying, and from the repetition of wiping tables and cooker sur-faces and food from little faces. I'm a thousand little pieces inside but it's changing because the walking, and the sight of the boys on bikes, has calmed some of that unease and irritation rattling inside me.

I walk fast, gulping in the warm air, but I'm going nowhere. I stop on the track, tipping my head back to look up at the endless blue sky. When I look down, I see a bumblebee slowly crossing the track at my feet. Despite the hugeness of the landscape we are in, and the endless twist of white ribbon of the chalk path ahead of me, the bee is very small but very vivid, mov-ing slowly through the dust. I pause and look down at it, remembering the boy staring into the ground beneath his BMX wheels as if he could see something there that mattered, as if he was also looking at a reflec-tion of himself. The bee seems huge and I watch it reflected in my sunglasses, rather than through the lenses themselves. Perhaps it senses my shadow above it, because something makes it stop, pausing amongst the dust and flecks of flint which must feel like boulders around it. It seems to react to my presence, recoiling from my gaze as if it has an emotional life. Very, very gently, I lay my palm flat on the ground, five inches from the bee. Does it breathe out? Does it breathe a sigh of relief? It moves forward, edging towards me so that moments later the bee is sitting on the back of my hand. Its tiny wings are closed around it like a gossamer film of protection; they are so vulnerable: I think of Lester and something in my heart lurches.

At that moment, I meet myself again. Because even though the tiny bee is sitting on my hand, and the sky is huge and blue and so warm all around me, and I am, underneath it all, quite happy, what I want now is to lie down on the track and feel my arms cut on the flints that lie on the path. I'd like to see my crimson blood mixing with the dust like rain falling on dry concrete and giving it that particular smell. I'd like my body to become a part of the earth beneath me. I want to bleed into the earth, my backbone scraping against the stones. I want to feel everything around me and inside me, too. I want to open my body to all the terror and all the life that's contained in the landscape.

I think of the boys on bikes, because they must have made it to Wayland's Smithy now. The thought of them there, oblivious, spitting into the earth, makes me feel alive and relieved that life cannot ever be contained by good behaviour, or even zero tolerance. I hope they are making a fire there, near the sign where it says 'NO FIRES', and sitting beneath the cathedral of beech trees close to the sign that says 'NO PUBLIC RIGHT OF WAY'. I hope they are feeling the ancient ways around them. I press my hand back against the earth; the bee crawls across my palm, tentatively, then back on to the warm ground. I go back home, to the abundant joy.

Sometimes I have to remind myself: You wanted this! You wanted messy and you wanted a full plate.

And the voice in my head says: Is this messy enough? Is your plate full enough now?

Yes, it's full now.

Until I had Lester, I experienced an irrational emptiness, a strange, unsatisfied hunger, which was shaped exactly like a child, which crept up on me when each baby reached a few months old. It didn't happen straight away, when I was wrapped up in the tiny baby in my arms, but it would silently slide into me just at the moment when that baby started moving away from me. When the baby could sit up and crawl, and feed himself using a plastic cup or a spoon, and she could spend a day without me, I felt a need to go back to the start and create it all again.

I've never been able to plan my family around practical details, like the question of whether we could actually afford another baby, or whether we had a house big enough, or what kind of car we might drive with so many children. Somehow the costs of more children get assimilated: the children all share bedrooms and one another's clothes, and I'm fairly relaxed about squashing them into a car that's never quite big enough.

All those concerns seem prosaic compared to the need to take myself back again, to the beginning of life, back to the baby. Back to the centre, the golden core. It's like an addict's hunger. I crave the feeling of holding my absolutely new baby; I'm intoxicated by the softness of a new baby's head in my palm, the soft, incomparably sweet sight of tiny eyes opening, the little limbs folded against my body, the tug on my breasts of a baby feeding. I'm giddy in the love I've felt for all my children, too. It's the purest and most intense kind of love. I can't get enough of it.

I've craved the cosmic weirdness of childbirth, the screaming fear and pain, the agonizing ecstasy of labour. I wanted to step back into the realm of life and death colliding, which is my experience of giving birth to my children. Childbirth took me to the brink of my own human experience; it was terrifying and it was extraordinary, this sense that I'd looked at death as a way of showing me what it felt like to truly be alive. It was the biggest, darkest frontier I'd ever taken myself to; pushing myself to that brink feels to me like the very reason I was put on this planet.

I knew that these things would bring with them a shattering, too, of the person I was and the life I was carefully regaining as the baby grew away from me. But I wanted that. It was a way of destroying myself without dying. I wanted to be shattered.

Five children have completely satisfied me and completely shattered me. I need to find myself again amongst our children. I need to wrestle time back under control, and to still this whirring sense that my life is perpetually out of control.

When Lester was a newborn baby, I lay on the bed with him and felt as though time shimmered like a kinetic force in the sunlight of my bedroom, and the older children were just a sound in a faraway playroom. I wanted to be there for Lester, to be able to sit quietly, with just him; I knew that each moment with this lovely baby was priceless. His life was happening entirely in the present tense: look away from him, and I would miss a moment of him. I could not waste that, because if I didn't concentrate on all parts of him, I felt I was throwing shards of gold into the mud. Being a mother to a newborn made me feel that I needed to gather up all those little shards and heap them together, so precious, and stare at them, so that they made up my baby's face. I could not squander them.

But this feeling of the stillness of life around a newborn baby scared me, too. As soon as I willed time to stand still in order to feel each of those prized moments, it started to terrify me. It looked like midsummer outside, but my world inside rattled at the windows as though there was a storm indoors. The storm told me that time standing still was no good, as it meant my life was over. In those motionless moments, it was as if I was lost. And now I wish I could step back to that moment, so recent, and also a lifetime ago, and scoop myself out of it, lift myself up to look at the point where I am now and say, See, there was nothing to be afraid of. Sometimes motherhood submerges you, but you can come up for air, and you are still here. Shattered, but there's space to put yourself back together.

As Lester moves further away from his life as a baby, I feel a gathering sense of urgency to realize myself as the person I am alongside the person I am as a mother. The maternal and personal twist together like ivy and myrtle bound around one another to form a wreath. As a mother I am ivy, strong and dark green and everywhere; but who I am as someone separate from the children is more fragile. It's the pale green leaves of myrtle which the ivy will suffocate if I let it.

And as Lester approaches his first year on this earth, Jimmy walks through the last days of his exams. He's serious in a way I've never seen before, focused on the work, much more organized as he prepares his school bag before each test. Afterwards he emerges, blinking, grinning, touching adulthood.

'It's all right, Mum,' he says. 'We got through, see?'

I don't want to stop working but it's 2.45 p.m. I'm sitting at the kitchen table, trying to fashion some words I have written into real ideas inside real sentences.

Upstairs, I can hear Lester waking, banging his bottle on the edge of his cot as he calls for me, or anyone, to lift him out. I've only just hit my stride with my work, but the primary school day is about to end. It's time to get the kids from school.

Lester bobs on my hip in the sunshine as we scoop up Dash first, who is clasping a large piece of paper covered with drying purple paint. 'It's a jellyfish peeping out at the night sky,' he tells me, which I hadn't realized. Then he says, 'I wish I was a T. Rex,' as I buckle him in, and we talk about which animals have the most exciting lives.

At the school gate, waiting for Evangeline, I feel a familiar sense of longing for her. There's a blur of parents, grandparents, childminders in flip-flops, carrying lunch boxes, balancing babies on hips, bumping into one another as they bend down. One mother jangles a set of keys in the face of a baby, a few months old, who has started to squirm and fuss in his buggy, bored of waiting for the teachers and children to come out; others make plans for the summer holidays.

Across the schoolyard I catch sight of Evangeline, and I feel my heart lurch watching her sweet, serious face as she looks for me. In that moment her love is the only thing I need. It's every part of my identity and it's the reason I'm alive. It's the planets aligning to make up the universe. It's good and truth put together. For this moment, being a mother is the only thing in the world I need: it is the expression of my greatest joy.

'I'm so glad you chose me as your baby,' Evangeline sighs into my arms. And as we drive home she asks me what I've been doing and I tell her I'm writing a book about being a mum. I watch the small slice of her face in the rear-view mirror. She looks out of the window, thinking about what I have said, then flicks her eyes back to me in the mirror.

'That's funny you're writing a book about being a mum,' she says. 'It's funny, because a lot of times being a mum is just taking me and Dash to swimming or wait-ing outside ballet. Mum, what's for supper?'

Alex messages me. She wants to tell me herself, before I hear it from a friend, but she's moving. To a university town, over three hours away, to be closer to her mother and stepfather, so that she can train to be a clinical psy-chologist. Her mother's going to help out with her daughters and she's found a house to rent. Her husband's looking for a new job. It's a new chapter in their lives.

I feel a conflicted pull between relief for her, and sadness that my close friend, whom I've shared much of my motherhood with, is leaving. But I understand that after several years of being a full-time mother she wants something else, too.

'I thought that if I gave everything to them, there might be nothing left of me when they are teenagers leaving home,' she tells me. 'I've realized that I can't give every part of myself to motherhood without losing too much. I need to reclaim myself.'

Alex is right. Having a child is like being given the most precious and beautiful thing in the entire world. It's yours, absolutely, and to start with you must not let it out of your sight, except for short periods. It's fragile and perfect and magic, but also heavy and difficult to care for. You must look after this wondrous thing, and nurture it all of the time, until you can spend longer and longer apart from it. And then one day you must give it away, out to the world. Having looked after it for a long time, the only certainty you have is that you will lose it. It won't be yours any more.

This is shocking.

It's also a relief.

Seeing Alex move onwards makes me feel less guilty about going away from Lester, from all of the children, to work. I increase Pavel's hours, so that soon I'm working four full days a week. One day, I email Yasna about a job. Her email returns with an out-of-office that she's on surrogate leave. We talk, a few days later. Yes, it's true! She laughs. She's having twins, by surrogate. 'Two girls!' she says, and I sense her excitement in those words, because although she loves her boys, she had also desperately wanted a girl. And she tells me she is stepping away from work for a bit. 'Darling. We'll meet soon. For now, I need to really look at motherhood.'

★

When Lester is one, Dolly and Evangeline make an elaborate plan of baking him a cake. They scatter coloured hundreds and thousands all over the kitchen and leave the sink full of buttery pans. I help them ice it, whipping up sugary white icing which slides across the hot cake. Dolly spells out 'Everyone Loves Lester' in spidery writing. Afterwards I watch Dash and Lester splash in the paddling pool, scooping up handfuls of dried grass to float there.

'Creatures!' says Dash. 'Me and Lester have made swimming creatures!'

At teatime we gather together in the kitchen, Pete leaving his work and Jimmy returning early from the lake, where he'd vanished earlier with friends and his inflatable dinghy. I close the curtains – Dash insists we must make it dark – as Dolly bears the cake, candles flaming, to Lester, sitting up at the table now, and our voices join together in a chorus of small but crucial celebration. All eyes are on Lester, who smiles, looking at us all, surprised, but registering quite clearly this first big moment in our big, messy family that's just for him. He's luminous and beautiful, a child emerging.

When the candles are out, the cake devoured, Pete goes back to work and Dolly vanishes upstairs to her room, and Dash and Evangeline spill back outside into the garden and the day moves onwards. Jimmy stays in the kitchen, helping me clear up the plates. The trip to the lake has not been successful.

'We got told off,' he says, rinsing plates in the sink.

I pause. 'Why? Were you doing something wrong?'

'We were told not to go on the lake in the dinghy because we might fall in.'

'You what?'

'We might fall in,' he replies, flicking water from the ends of his fingertips and then running his hands through his hair.

'But isn't that the whole point of going out on a lake in a dinghy when you're a teenager? Falling in?'

'Yeah, well, I thought so. Sometimes, when you're a teenager, it feels like there's always an adult there telling you off, whatever you do.'

Later on, I go up on to White Horse Hill, just with Jimmy. It's dusk, an almost cloudless evening. Jimmy thrusts his hands in his pockets, loping in front of me with Pablo, who runs beside him. I can really see him now, my growing son, walking ahead of me and away from me. Seeing him growing out of family life is painful but it's sort of miraculous, too. As he jogs ahead, I think of walking with him, out in the country, when he was Dash's age, when he jumped into puddles and wanted to be carried and was always losing his shoes, always barefoot, full of electric energy.

I am seeing who he really is more and more now. Sometimes I am so pressed up tight against the younger children that I feel I can barely catch a sense of their outlines before they change again. They slip through my hands, even as they stand right in front of me. And their chaos means that being with them is sometimes like inhabiting the inside of a dishwasher, churning around and around.

There's a special sort of stillness which comes with the company of an almost-adult child. I feel intensely grateful for Jimmy. I've got so much wrong in my mothering: my impatience and frustration, my desire to escape, my anger which bubbles up out of nowhere when I'm feeling bad, the way I shout and that disconnected sense I sometimes have when I'm with them that I'm not actually present in the room. And Jimmy has tested me, and there will be more tests to come, I'm sure, but that's OK. I can see a way through now.

It's still and hot: high summer. Yellow light seeps across the burnt-yellow hills, and Jimmy pauses on the track ahead of me. I catch up with him just as the dipping sunset throws some last brilliant rays over the golden field of corn ahead of us. There are some round marks in the field, lying in between the wide tram lines. Crop circles, maybe, Jimmy says hopefully, because which teenage boy doesn't love a good conspiracy theory?

We watch the sun shimmer behind the horizon, speculating on how a crop circle might actually be made. Planks and pieces of string, outside in the middle of the night, and a lot of patience, suggests Jimmy.

I don't want to be anywhere other than here, with him.

'It's the kind of thing you like doing, isn't it, Mum?' And then he tells me that's what makes me a good mum. 'Because you wear black and gold trainers but you also like doing old-fashioned things like being outside in a field at night-time. Stuff like that.' I want to laugh. I wish I'd known it was all so simple.

'I love you, Jimmy,' I say quickly.

'Love you too, Mum,' he says over his shoulder, then he walks ahead again, the silence creating a gap between us as if this honesty has shocked us both a bit.

And as he walks further away from me into the thickening dusk, I watch him getting smaller, realizing that all the moments of motherhood I have lived through with him lead here, to this perfect instant of feeling together but also quite distinct from each other, and also separating, separating, separating from one another all the time.

It hurts.

A skylark cries above us as Jimmy suddenly starts jogging, the space getting bigger as he leaves me behind, and he's calling Pablo, who jumps and dances and runs beside him. And I have to stop because I am almost winded with a breathless sense of certainty that while my love for Jimmy will always grow, the spaces between us will get bigger and bigger. Is this what being a mother really feels like, in the end? This sense that your child will walk further and further away from you? Is this what all those moments of motherhood have led to? This sense of loss?

I want to reach out and shout to Jimmy to tell him to stop, to come back, to pull him close so that we can go back to the beginning and start again. The light is changing as we walk, the brightness altering so that the few long streaks of cloud in the sky look like silver shards of light slicing through the dark pink glow of the evening.

'Jimmy, look!' I call to him, and he spins round to face me. 'Look at the clouds, Jimmy.'

He laughs, tipping his face up to the brilliant, changing sky; then he looks back towards me, raising his hand as though he's telling me something. But I can't hear, and he whistles to Pablo. He looks away and keeps walking. I look away, to the distant valley below, where a train moves quickly through the landscape, then vanishes.

When I look back at the chalk path snaking ahead of me, Jimmy is already reaching the top of the hill. I feel the last warmth of the evening joining with all this love which surrounds us, and I realize that he's so far ahead of me now I can hardly see him any more.

Epilogue

A friend who is an artist living in Stornoway sent me a video she had made of multi-coloured ribbons tied to a barbed-wire fence, blowing wildly in the wind. It was mesmerizing to watch, but also frustrating: I wanted to reach inside the video and grasp the ribbons, to enjoy their bright satin colours in my hand and hold them still.

When I look backwards to the time before Lester's birth, and further back, before all their births, I see that labour sent me to a wide but separate world; sometimes I didn't come back from that place for months, even years. Mothering a baby changed me. I lost myself, out there in the wilderness. The world around felt closed off from me, as I was closed in myself. I realize that the wilderness was inside me. The dark valleys were places I had to cross alone. Motherhood tests my mettle every day; it needs me to be brave all the time. Now, though, I realize the fortitude that motherhood demands of me also *makes* me: I lost myself in labour, but now Lester is almost three I am more myself than ever before.

Lester is no longer a baby. He is like an animal who can suddenly speak, as if Pablo had started talking to me. We have conversations; mostly he likes talking about motorbikes and monster trucks, and what a million balls in a room would look like. He has moved out of his cot into a bed of his own. Sometimes in the early morning I go and lie close to him, to watch him, daring myself to see if I can actually witness him growing before my eyes. He sleeps with his head thrown back, the red bow of his mouth slightly open. I stroke him in his sleep; his legs are so warm and smooth as silk. He has inherited Dash's biscuit smell of boyhood. He knows the words to both *Where the Wild Things Are* and *Are You My Mummy?* off by heart. This makes me relieved: the time I gave him had an impact, even if he cannot remember it.

Sometimes I think motherhood is like looking through different-coloured lenses to change your view of each day. Sometimes these lenses are dark, unfocused, confusing to look through; they make me want to look away. Motherhood can be depressing. At other times they are smudgy and buttery, covered with dirty fingerprints that constantly need cleaning. That's the school run and pasta-for-supper-again lenses. But sometimes memory and happiness come together at the same time for a moment, and then the lenses are clear and sparkling, and frustration, boredom, irritation vanish and I feel nothing but the absolute joy of knowing the children and loving them.

Dash still likes to be naked for long parts of every day. He bird-watches and also runs around the house with a dead mouse in a box, furious, spurting tears when I try to take it from him, stamping his naked body. 'But I love it! It's beautiful and strokable!' Starting school delights him. Admiring his new grey nylon trousers and royal-blue sweatshirt in a mirror, he puts his hands into his pockets, announcing to me that now, he is a wondrous schoolboy.

I have come to understand that love for my children is not something I experience in a single trajectory. It is not a constant note. At exactly the time that it demands that I be ceaselessly strong and present, it also leaves me in a state of raw vulnerability. Some days I feel so much anger mixed with my love I have to leave the room. It is elastic. Mother love contains everything, all the frustration and all the joy.

Watching Evangeline as she climbs the steps of the big coach parked outside the playground, heading off on a school trip, sends my mind backwards to Mum waving me off on a trip with a red plastic Snoopy lunch box. When I opened it on my lap on the bus, revealing my lunch (brown-bread sandwiches with Marmite, a peeled carrot, Frazzles and a Penguin biscuit) I felt homesick for her. I wanted to get off the bus and go back to her. I long for Evangeline in the same way; her smile cracks my heart. When I am with her I want to gulp her down; she is so beautiful and so loving. She is inventive too, always a coloured felt-tip pen in her hand, drawing beds for her babies. 'Memories go from your head to your heart for ever,' she whispers at me hotly when I nuzzle the back of her neck.

You cannot be a mother and not feel a tangible sense of sadness about time gone. But I am also realizing that nothing is lost: everything my children and I have shared, everything we have done, is with us, safe in the box of the past we carry inside, always. The feeling of their hands squeezing mine as we walk through the long grass, or their slippery wet bodies as they jump from the edge of the bath into my arms, or the pudginess of their sticky cheeks as I kiss them, or the distant, frightening beauty of their faces when I watch them while they are sleeping, is something that will always be there.

Dolly bounds along; she grows and grows; she is taller than me. I watch her in a play. She tells me she loves drama more than anything because it's a way of expressing herself. 'It's how I feel and live pure emotion,' she explains. After the play she is exhilarated by what she has achieved. She is almost sixteen; my daughter is at the centre of the stage now, and I'm watching, applauding from the big audience as light shines on to her.

Their childhoods will end; Dolly is following Jimmy and hers is almost gone. I feared this so much because my experience of being mothered ended when I was sixteen; but now I can see that the love I have given them will go on. I had an irrational fear, contained within my memories of what happened to my mother, that it would end violently. And it *will* change, it must, but it won't stop. It's like the sound of wind in the branches of that cathedral of trees on the Ridgeway. The wind moves amongst the trees, expanding to fill the space. The trees are always there, solid, an arbour, but the wind shifts and changes, then whooshes onwards. That sound is liberating. It is thrilling.

After GCSEs, Jimmy went to sixth-form college for his A levels; soon he will be leaving, to go to art school. We have talked and talked and talked and talked; we have also shouted at each other a lot. Sworn a fair bit. Once, he made me so angry I threw a cowboy boot right at him with all my force because I wanted to hurt him. Still, we went on talking. We fought and talked, argued and talked some more. He often continues to evade me, vanishing into the fields around our home in pursuit of hedonistic liberties. Telling a teenager they cannot do the things you have done does not work; instead, I have learned to give him the freedoms he wants in return for his honesty. We have also bonded over Louis Theroux documentaries and his growing penknife collection. He's no longer a child. We have passed through all four seasons of parenting together, as if spring, summer, autumn and winter in our relationship as mother and son have gone, and now a completely new year has started.

Sometimes, while he is still living at home, I go into his room at night and the window is open. I don't run my hands under his pillows any more. I don't read the notebook he's left open on the desk. The curtains may be moving slightly. He's not there, and his sheets are rumpled. It's like he's just flown, out and away. And I think of the younger children, and the tangle of fear about what I might get wrong with them, or the amount of work I still have to do for them: the spelling tests, the swimming lessons and bedtime reading that await me; the quantity of packed lunches I still have to make; and the hours and hours and hours I will have to wait at the school gate. I don't want to miss any opportunities for them. It's a lot of pressure. But then I see Jimmy, right at the end of childhood, and I know he is definitely happy. We got that right together. I mean, it's one thing to grow up to be a doctor, or an architect or a writer or a teacher, but to be happy? That's really difficult.

I could not bear the separation from Pete that our life as parents demands if I didn't know that who we are together will always be there, later, when they are all grown up. Marriage is long but it's also precious. I do not want to be rough with it. Loving one person, commitment, isn't boring. It's bigger and better than falling in love. It's earth-shattering, every day. It's everything.

And when I look at our children all I know, with absolute certainty, is that I do not believe in developmental charts any more. The best, the most valuable things I can give them are my love and my time, and they will choose the path they must take, in their own way. Really, it doesn't matter when your baby rolls over, or walks, talks, reads. It doesn't matter how fast they grow up: it will all happen.

So do not wrap them up too tight. Life will hurt them a lot, that's absolutely certain, and since you cannot prevent that, instead you should show them how to be brave. Teach them to swim but then allow them to fall in the lake without being told off. Remind them what danger is but do not worry when they cut their hands on knives. Encourage them to live, expansively. Let your children play with fire.

Acknowledgements

When Lester was a few weeks old, I tried to find a book that would help me make more sense of my emotions. I already had four children – this was not my first rodeo – but the intensity of mothering five children was sometimes shocking.

I was often a zombie: I was totally spaced out and my head could not revolve fast enough to speak to my children when they needed me, usually simultaneously, with wildly different needs. I had been a mother for fifteen years when Lester was born, but I felt as far from an expert as it is possible to be. It made me remember, again, that mothering is something you never really master, but – at least in my experience – always blunder through as though you've lost the instructions.

The extremities of new motherhood surprised me, once again. If a new job had made me feel like this, I'd definitely have been asking my boss for an urgent review, or at least a big pay rise. More than at any point since I'd first had a child, I wanted to read what other women thought and felt about motherhood. I wanted to know if the feelings I was having were the ones other women were having, too, and I didn't want a book purely about what it feels like to be the mother to a baby or young child, as that was only a small part of the story. Pregnancy and post-natal weirdness are just the very start of motherhood, although they are where a lot of books about motherhood also end.

So I started asking friends and other women I met both in real life and through social media what they really felt about the experience of mothering. 'What does motherhood feel like?' was the question I kept returning to, and I started writing about my own feelings. Lester was still a new baby, neither Dash nor Evangeline were at full-time school, and Jimmy and Dolly were both in their mid-teens. It was a bewildering, passionate, exhausting, sticky, dark, beautiful time, and I wanted to try to capture some of it before that particular phase of my life had passed.

Motherhood is a difficult thing to write about. It's often boring and repetitive, and although I wanted to capture some sense of that, it was also the last thing I wanted the experience of reading my book to be. Neither did I want the book to be an anecdotal record of cute funny things my kids have said and done, because, seriously, who wants to read that? Instead I wanted to try to answer that question – what does motherhood feel like? – and record the extremities of its highs and lows. Nothing else makes me as angry as motherhood does; nothing makes me as happy.

If you've read *My Wild and Sleepless Nights*, you will know that it's very confessional and deeply personal. I am not trying to answer this question for everyone, but I hope that in being honest about my own experiences, other women might find some of their own reflected, too.

Since finishing this book, my concept of motherhood has continued to change. I'm less of a zombie than I was when Lester was tiny, though I am, regrettably, often a banshee. I do not have a baby any more, and shortly after this book will be published, Jimmy will no longer be a teenager, either. Life changes. Motherhood slips past, elusive, baffling, profound.

While the friends I have depicted in the book are real, I have changed salient details of their lives, for anonymity. A silent thank-you to those three women – you know who you are – who were so generous in sharing their thoughts, and so open to being re-created on the page.

I am also very grateful to certain people who read early, messy versions of my manuscript. Hannah Thomas and Amy Shuckburgh gave me notes and encouragement in between their own school runs, and Jessie Brinton read through my descriptions of birth just after giving birth herself. Thanks to Raffaella Barker for a brisk reading when I needed it most. Antonia Quirke and Natasha Lunn tacitly encouraged me, in ways they probably don't know, to keep on writing. I am grateful to Gill Hall at Childrey Cafe, who gave me a quiet space in a back room to work, away from the chaos of my own kitchen. I am indebted to Gillian Stern, for both her deep friendship and her complete brilliance when it comes to editing formless words into a shape. Thank you to Liz Gilbert for dropping a spark of light into my palms on a dark day. And love and thanks to my stepmother Alexandra Pringle, for so many important things in my life, including the encouragement she gave me when she read the finished manuscript. I'm also grateful to her for running Rick's call centre so efficiently and gracefully. And big, big thanks to Benedicta Bywater, for many insightful, inspiring, virtual conversations which have helped me at crucial moments.

My agent Kirsty McLachlan was endlessly encouraging, and especially enthusiastic during my early conception of this book.

Working with the team at Transworld has been a complete joy; creating a book is about so much more than purely the written words, and I feel incredibly grateful to Susanna Wadeson, Helena Gonda and Alison Barrow, who have all contributed so much to the process. Thanks also to Kate Samano, Richenda Todd, Alice Murphy-Pyle and Marianne Issa El-Khoury, and to Anna Morrison, who created the beautiful cover which represents what the inside of my head often feels like.

I am amazed by the generosity of my husband Pete, and without him I am clear that I could not have written this book. He read all the early writing and helped me so much in shaping it. I know that some of the things I have written about have been hard for him to read, but he is always encouraging and always inspiring, at the same time that he is tough and loving. He has said to me that he might not like everything I write, but that he will always defend my right to express myself. My relationship with him is a kind of miracle in my life that has changed everything for me.

Most of all, I would like to acknowledge my children: Jimmy, Dolly, Evangeline, Dash and Lester. Because my writing is confessional and personal, and I have written so openly about the children, I have been talking to them about some of it while I was working. Dolly has read parts of it. Jimmy has read everything that is about him; I know there are other parts of the book he wouldn't want to read. He read the final draft of the sections about him on a bus journey to college. Afterwards, he texted me back: *Just finished the email you sent. I'm happy with everything you've written and I think you write really really well. You're an AMAZING mother and always will be no matter what. Not just because of what you do for us but because you're OUR mum xxxxxxxx*

I hope that if the children do ever look back at *My Wild and Sleepless Nights* when they are older, they will read it as a portrait of my complete love for them. The darkness I describe is mine alone..